ENDORSEMENTS

Dr. Daniel and Jennifer Vassell, graduates of the Marriage and Family Counseling Program at the Pentecostal Theological Seminary, Cleveland, TN, are well qualified and seasoned marriage counselors. In their latest book, *The Epic Marriage*, they offer fresh and insightful information for married couples who choose not to settle for the status quo or average marriage, but desire to experience the full joy of marital bliss through empowerment of the Holy Spirit. It's a must read for couples, and a great teaching resource that churches and therapists can utilize to strengthen the richness of marriage.

—Dr. Michael L. Baker
Chancellor of Education, Church of God; and
President, Pentecostal Theological Seminary
Cleveland, TN

Dr. Daniel Vassell is an amazing gift to the body of Christ. This book, being coauthored by Dr. Daniel and Jenny Vassell, is indeed a clarion call to married couples. As he states, "The quality of a marriage is not measured by how it began, but by how it is nurtured and sustained." This book is just that—the aid needed to sustain the quality and depth of a marriage relationship. Marriage can be seen as two imperfect people trying to build a perfect union—but this is impossible—because, trying to create this perfect union will be the cause of endless frustration. Daniel and Jenny provide for us some tools to make the marriage better—or EPIC as they call it.

Delve into this book and discover together what the potential of an EPIC marriage model may add to your marriage union. I simply love the way they add the absolute necessity of the role the Holy Spirit plays or needs to play to make your marriage EPIC. I remember growing up with a plaque in our home saying,

"A family that prays together; stays together." Daniel and Jenny highlight this point with much more clarity.

Enjoy the journey of discovering your EPIC marriage.

—Dr. Stafford W. Petersen
General Moderator
Full Gospel Church of God
South Africa

Dr. Daniel and Jenny Vassell coauthored this very relevant resource—*The Epic Marriage: The Spirit-Empowered Life*. It is a realistic look at marriage, dismissing the myths while providing efficient examples and sound spiritual insight.

Every chapter offers a powerful awareness into what it takes to make your marriage not just last but thrive. From the first chapter, "Epic Marriage Foundation," to the last chapter, "The Ravishing Lovers," the advice given in this book is bound to make a difference if it is heeded to.

This manuscript offers hope to the despondent and courage to those who might have become complacent in their relationship. The review questions at the end of each chapter aids in reinforcing the wisdom given. I agree with the Vassells, having an epic marriage is a matter of choice; it is possible to have a sustaining, enduring love that can weather the storms of life. This is an excellent resource workbook for marriage counselors and married couples as well.

—Dr. Annette Lazarus-Rose,
Lead Pastor and Presiding Bishop,
Bethesda Healing Center,
Brooklyn, New York

Daniel and Jennifer Vassell have given the Church and the world a rare treasure in their book, *The Epic Marriage*. They have successfully woven a tapestry of scholarship, both biblical and psychological, along with practical and honest insight into the institution of marriage. The genius of the book is that it makes a potentially complicated and difficult subject readily accessible and extremely understandable to the contemporary 21st-century reader in a way that is particularly useful. The honesty of the book will appeal especially to millennials who often are suspicious of religious literature as "fake"; here, traditionally tabooed issues are frankly addressed in a Christian and competent way. Counselors, parents, and pastors will find *The Epic Marriage* to be a rich resource, and anyone who seeks to enrich their marriage and those of their beloved community will find it *real* and relevant.

—Dr. Samuel Vassel and Angela Vassel
Lead Pastor and wife (counselor)
Bronx, Bethany Church of the Nazarene

The Bible depicts marriage as the first and foundational institution upon which all other institutions are built. But let's face it, marriage can be exhausting. Marriage can be delightful, and yet filled with challenges.

In the book, *The Epic Marriage: The Spirit-Empowered Life*, Dr. Daniel Vassell and his wife, Jenny Vassell, have shared with us the wisdom needed to move marriages from merely surviving to beautifully thriving, and to become epic marriages. The word epic refers to something that is impressive, monumental, and awesome.

This book points us to the source of epic marriages—which are relationships lived out in a Spirit-empowered life. In Ephesians 5, before Paul the apostle highlights how biblical relationships should function, he calls upon us to "be filled with the Spirit" (Ephesians 5:18 NKJV). It is only after this admonition that Paul speaks to us about loving husbands and happy wives.

The Epic Marriage: The Spirit-Empowered Life reminds us that it is only when we are living a Spirit-empowered life that we can have loving relationships which will lead to the epic marriage.

If you long for a marriage filled with love, joy, and contentment, *The Epic Marriage: The Spirit-Empowered Life* will provide the insights needed to move your marriage to epic proportions. This book is filled with practical information and provides thought-provoking questions which will help couples evaluate their relationships so as to take the necessary steps to both an epic marriage and a Spirit-empowered life.

Every engaged, newlywed, and veteran couple will benefit from the wisdom and sound advice found in this book. Epic relationships are fundamental to strong families, churches, and nations, so let us cultivate epic marriages that are Spirit-empowered by utilizing the message found in *The Epic Marriage: The Spirit-Empowered Life*.

—Bishop Woodroe Thompson
Administrative Bishop
Church of God of Prophecy—Eastern Canada

In *The EPIC Marriage*, Christian leaders and authors, Daniel and Jenny Vassell, have gifted God's church and married couples everywhere. From Adam and Eve to Solomon and from "Partner-Focus Petitionary Prayer" to an exegesis of Old Testament Hebrew terms, this volume is both scriptural and personal to the reader while providing practical strategies to strengthen and enhance the spiritual/physical union that is marriage.

An "EPIC" marriage is idealistic, but not at all unrealistic. It is attainable and worth the effort. Indeed, marriages termed "failed" are termed thusly, precisely because they are not "anchored" in a love relationship with God or His Word. As a work, *The EPIC Marriage* is indeed anchored in the love of God, His Word, and in the essential empowerment of the Holy Spirit to truly provide a marriage characterized by love, respect, and genuine contentment. This is a straightforward and practical book meant for married couples whose desire is to love God and reflect that love in the unselfish and fulfilling relationship they have with their own spouse . . . their sweetheart.

We recommend this text to all who honestly desire to enjoy an EPIC marriage!

—Dr. O. Wayne and Rev. Pamela R. Brewer
International Directors of Men's Discipleship
and Women's Discipleship
Church of God International Offices
Cleveland, Tennessee

This book is not only a "must read" for every couple, but also a "manual for the best" in a husband and wife relationship. *The Epic Marriage: The Spirit-Empowered Life* takes you from the ground of marriage to the highest level of a love relationship between a man and a woman led by the Holy Spirit. It allows you to drink the principles of "epic lovers" who want to understand why God created men and women. From Adam and Eve to Solomon and the Shulamite woman, and from everyday life to the internal love in body chemistry, Dr. Daniel Vassell and his lovely wife, Jennifer Vassell, take all readers back to the intended purpose of the sacred covenant between husband and wife. The taste of paradise is real when couples apply the principles written in this book. All satisfaction guaranteed!!!

—Bishop Jean T. and Denise L. Tshiteya
Lead Pastor of The New Jerusalem
Church of God in Liège, Belgium
Church of God Western Europe
Youth and Discipleship Director

For anyone who has had the distinct pleasure of meeting Dr. Daniel and Jenny Vassell, have had an opportunity to experience their ministry through the books they have written, or the initiatives they have led, you can attest to their genuine and passionate commitment to educating, equipping, and empowering couples and families to live their best lives now! *The Epic Marriage* is yet another masterful resource for couples to explore the treasures that lie within their marriage.

While many books have been written about marriage, this book provides foundational and functional attributes that couples can use to restore, enhance, equip, and apply to their relationship in a simple, yet intentional way. From the Scriptural references, real-life stories, statistical and psychological information, to the review questions at the end of each chapter, the readers can resolve that this book was written with them in mind.

With their many years of research, experience, and counseling, Dr. Daniel and Jenny Vassell have addressed the many layers of marriage identifying misconceptions and key challenges that are common to most couples. Through educating in the areas of love, prayer, service, communication, commitment, intimacy, joy, happiness, and Spirit-living, couples will appreciate both the spiritual and natural perspectives presented, which provides answers for epic marital success. Both husbands and wives will find a refreshing comprehensive dialogue that encourages self-evaluation and stirs motivation to invest in their roles in their relationship.

For couples aspiring to have "the epic marriage," this book will be the handbook that you can refer to for many years on your marital journey. We can truly say with confidence that this book carries a unique ability to invigorate and transform the marriages of all who will read it. It has been our pleasure to read this latest text on marriage and to write this endorsement for our mentors whose relationship has inspired us to love and serve one another more deeply.

—Dr. Shawn and Caleen Howard,
District Overseer, North York, Ontario
Founder and Lead Pastor
Life Changers Church
Authors, *7 Love Keys to a Successful Marriage:
Principles for a Lasting Relationship"*

This is a life-changing book. No one marries with the intention to suffer, yet there are many sick marriage relationships. *The Epic Marriage* written by Dr. Daniel and Jenny Vassell is the ANSWER for a loving, desired relationship.

—Apostle Kevin and Sweety Permal
Lead pastors and Presiding Bishop
Light Ministries International
President of Federation of Pentecostal Churches in Mauritius, Africa

If there were ever two persons whom I think are particularly qualified to write on marriage, it would be Daniel and Jenny Vassell. Knowing them from when we were young people, living in their homes on numerous occasions, all the time observing their love and commitment to each other and their children, I esteem them as exemplifying God's will for marriage.

The focus of the book—a call to married persons to depend on the Holy Spirit for a meaningful marriage—is novel, yet was always there as the preventative answer to divorce and marital breakdown. I am glad that the Vassells have the insight on the subject and the courage to honestly and boldly challenge people to do things God's way.

May this book be of significant benefit to those already married and young people contemplating marriage.

Congratulations, Dr. Daniel and Jenny Vassell.

—Rev. Donald A. Roberts, D.Min.
President, Bethel Bible College of the Caribbean—Jamaica
Director of Education, Church of God World Missions, Caribbean Region

In a day based on the stats, marriage has fallen on hard times; however, the Vassells continue to be drum majors for the power and pleasure of this divinely ordained arrangement we call marriage. Marriage certainly will stand the test of time regardless of the detractors. This is so, because it is a good thing; and it is a good thing, because it's a "God thing."

Kudos to the Vassells for one more relevant resource in their arsenal for the preservation of one of society's most vital anchors—covenant marriage.

—Bishop Earl Harrison
Lead Pastor
Mount Zion New Testament Church of God
St. Thomas, V.I. USA

The EPIC MARRIAGE

THE SPIRIT-EMPOWERED LIFE

The EPIC MARRIAGE

The Spirit-Empowered Life

Foreword by Dr. Oliver McMahan

Dr. Daniel and Jennifer Vassell

Unless otherwise noted, all Scripture quotations are taken from the *New King James Version* (NKJV). Copyright © 1979, 1980, 1982, 1990, 1995, Thomas Nelson Inc., Publishers. All rights reserved.

All quotation marked KJV are taken from the Holy Bible, King James Version.

All quotations marked ISV are taken from the *International Standard Version* (ISV). Copyright © 1995–2014 by ISV Foundation. ALL RIGHTS RESERVED INTERNATIONALLY. Used by permission of Davidson Press, LLC.

Scripture quotations marked NIV are taken from the Holy Bible, *New International Version* ®. NIV ®. Copyright © 1973, 1978, 1984, 2011 by Biblia, Inc. ®. Used by permission. All rights reserved worldwide.

Scripture quotations marked ESV are taken from the Holy Bible, *English Standard Version,* copyright © 2005. Used by permission of The Standard Bible Society, Wheaton, Illinois. All rights reserved.

Scripture quotations marked NET are taken from the NET Bible® Copyright © 1996–2006 by Biblical Studies Press, L.L.C. http://netbible.com. All rights reserved.

Scripture quotations marked HCSB are taken from the *Holman Christian Standard Bible.* Copyright © 1999, 2000, 2002, 2003, 2009 by Holman Bible Publishers, Nashville, Tennessee. All rights reserved.

Scripture quotations marked NASB are taken from the *New American Standard Bible.* Copyright © 1960, 1962, 1963, 1968, 1971, 1972, 1973, 1975, 1977, 1995 by The Lockman Foundation.

Scripture quotations marked AMPC are taken from the Amplified Bible, Classic Edition. Copyright © 1954, 1958, 1962, 1964, 1965, 1987 by The Lockman Foundation.

Scripture quotations marked DARBY are taken from the DARBY Translation of the Bible, which is now in Public Domain.

Scripture quotations marked Moffatt are taken from the Moffatt Translation of the Bible. Copyright © 1922, 1924, 1925, 1926, 1935 by Harper Collins; copyright © 1950, 1952, 1953, 1954 by James A.R. Moffatt. Reprinted in 1994 by Kregel Publications. All rights reserved.

ISBN: 978-1-7322962-8-2

ALL RIGHTS RESERVED: No part of this publication may be reproduced, stored in a retrieval system, or transmitted in any form or by any means—electronic, mechanical, photocopy, recording, or any other—except for brief quotations in printed reviews, without the prior permission of the copyright holder.

Copyright © 2018 by Dr. Daniel and Jennifer Vassell

Printed by Amazon

DEDICATION

This book is dedicated in honor of our late counseling professor and mentor, Dr. Douglas Slocomb, who served as the head of the Counseling Department of the Pentecostal Theological Seminary. He and his wife, Joyce, modeled the epic marriage life until the Lord took him home. Dr. Slocomb was not only an exemplary professor, but also both he and his wife took time to encourage couples globally to live epic marriages.

When I met with him to discuss this book project and requested that he write the foreword, he was excited. In that conversation, he reminded me that "epic marriage is not an event, but a process." He has since deceased, but he will always be remembered as a supporter and promoter of epic marriages.

To my parents, Evangelist William and Louise Vassell, whose 45 years of loving and committed relationship has not only inspired me but also served as a fitting example of an epic marriage. Thank you! Their relationship exemplified epic love—during difficult times, as well as happy times.

It is also dedicated to my loving and lovely wife and ministry companion, Jennifer Ann-Marie Mahalia Vernon-Vassell. She has lived out the epic life with me and is a coauthor of this book.

Finally, we dedicate this book to our son, James and his wife, Angela, and our daughter Aleah. As parents we are justly proud of our children who have submitted their lives to Christ and the guidance of Holy Spirit in their relationships.

TABLE OF CONTENTS

Foreword—Oliver McMahan 17

Preface 19

Acknowledgments 23

Introduction 25

Chapters

1. Epic Lovers' Marriage 31
2. Epic Marriage Foundation 61
3. A Love Promise Worth Keeping! 99
4. Communicating in Love 111
5. Diamond Love: Creative Use of Conflict 127
6. Joyful or Happy Lovers... 145
7. The Fearless Lover 165
8. The Delicate Lover 189
9. The Ravishing Lovers 211
10. Conclusion... 231

Answer Sheet 235

FOREWORD

Dr. Daniel and Jenny Vassell have put together an amazing book. It is very practical and relevant; in fact, the reader would be hard-pressed to find another volume that presents practical perspectives and accurate exercises for marriages today. Epic Marriage is not only a guide that is informative, but it is also a guide that helps you on the path.

The faith foundation of the book is incredible with correlations between the work of Christ and the Spirit to every facet challenging marriage today. The positive potential of God's power in a marriage, making it an "epic marriage," is sown throughout the book. The book blossoms and bears fruit in the heart and behavior of every couple who reads it, working through the exercises and challenges presented in the volume. Combined with the power of God's love in all aspects of married love, the Vassells seem to know exactly what couples face today, and specifically how God provides the answer.

Each chapter, from the definition of "Epic Lover's Marriage," to the "epic Marriage Foundation," the parts of marriage, the power of prayer, the "Compassion of Love," and all the way to specific applications, provides meaningful and workable solutions for marriages that are stuck in the anemia that robs couples of an epic marriage. Literally, from fearlessness, to delicateness, all the way to ravishing love, this book does it.

The EPIC MARRIAGE

The essential paradigm of the acrostic E-P-I-C:
- **E** – Empowered, Spirit-Living Encourager
- **P** – Partner-focused Petitionary Prayer
- **I** – Intimate Investor
- **C** – Compassionate Caregiver

sets the mold for Spirit-filled, Christ-realized marriage. This book is not theoretical or "pie in the sky" dreaming, but filled with real solutions for real problems.

Each scenario, such as "My Life or My Wife," and each diagram such as the cycle or men and women reacting in a spiral without love and without respect, presents a straightforward picture of what marriage can be. Each exercise plows through the mire of mediocrity and lifts a couple together to new levels of intimacy and godly love. Communication cycles, prayer perspectives, sexual intimacy, and many other challenges, opportunities, and marriage-building insights are all in this book.

Epic Marriage is an invitation to take your marriage from what it may have tragically become to what is achievable through sound, biblical, Spirit-led, and Christ-centered realities. Marriages that have not been making it, children who long for something better, a world that has been hurting, and a church filled with lifeless marriages all need to hear the message and the method of *Epic Marriage*.

—Oliver McMahan, Ph.D.
Professor of Counseling
Pentecostal Theological Seminary
Cleveland, TN

PREFACE

Why write a third book on marriage when there is a plethora, in fact, an oversaturation of books or manuals on the subject in the marketplace? The point is open for debate. The truth is, if it were up to us alone, another marriage book would not have been written. Matter of fact, I asked God not to have us write another marriage book. Why? Writing about marriage may give the wrong impression that we have it all together—that is far from the truth. The fact is, we have our own share of marital challenges. Writing about marriage tends to expose the vulnerabilities of its writers, but the Holy Spirit has impressed upon us to write it, and we have obeyed His voice. Finally, we wrote this book knowing full well that it has the capacity to be transformative—transforming both authors and readers into epic lovers.

A reader may say that was a good copout for an answer. No, if it were not for the Holy Spirit's leading, anointing, and inspiration, this project would not have been made possible.

So, what will our book add that is different from all other books on the market? I am glad you asked, but I will address this later. However, allow me to address the other marriage books that are on the market today.

In order to understand the character of these marriage books, we have categorized them under three headings:
    Self-help
    Marital Education
    Resources

To give us a better understanding about the marriage books on the market, I googled and reviewed the 90 top-selling books on the market. My review reveals that 46 were self-help and 44 educational. No resource book was listed in the top 90.

Self-help marriage manuals are written to provide couples with information that is aimed toward the building and enrichment of their marriages. The educational category provides information and knowledge from theology, bibliology, psychology, and other disciplines to enrich marriage education. And yes, the Christian church needs these kinds of writings to help anchor and fortify true Christian marriages, especially in this postmodern context. The third category, resources, includes books that address marriage counseling, including therapeutic practices and techniques. Many of these books deal with methods, skills, and techniques to address marital problems. Thank God for all these great writings, but one voice is still missing.

Our book is not written as a self-help, educational, or resource manual; instead, it is written as a clarion call to married couples to place their marriage to the disposal of the enabling power and presence of the Holy Spirit. It is the Holy Spirit who will help create, produce, and sustain a better-quality marriage, rather than depending exclusive on self-help books. Self-help and educational books are great complementary help along the way, but they are limited.

Learning about epic marriage does not create epic marriage. Learning to pray does not make us prayer warriors. Praying makes prayer warriors. Being indwelt and led by the Holy Spirit opens the door to living epic marriage lives.

Jenny and I do not confess nor pretend to have the prototypical epic marriage. But, we are allowing the Holy

Preface

Spirit on a daily basis to empower us in loving and compassionate service to each other, our children, and the community as a whole.

As you read this book, we are praying you will open up yourself and your marriage to experience the presence of the Holy Spirit; allow Him to invade your life and invite Him to become the center of your lives. Let Him indwell and empower you to be the epic lover you are created to be.

The EPIC MARRIAGE

ACKNOWLEDGMENTS

Many people have assisted us in the production of this book, and we cannot name them all. However, we would be remiss if we did not name a few people who have been instrumental in the creation of this project..

We would like to express our appreciation to our friend Bishop Wayne Vernon, the lead pastor of West Toronto Church of God, in Toronto, Canada. He has been one of our motivators and encouragers from the beginning. Wayne along with Dr. Cebert Adamson, and Simone Atungo have helped in doing much of the research and crafting of the framework of this book. Thank you for your time, effort, prayers, dedication and researching. You have become part of the cloud of witnesses encouraging the readers to seek for and live the epic marriage life.

Special thanks to my brother-in-law, Bishop Donovan Dyer, lead pastor of The Rock of Faith Worship Centre Church of God in Toronto, Canada, and a certified counselor for his help in reading and critiquing this book, as well as helping with the flow of the chapters.

Special thanks to James our son and his wife, Angela, for reading and giving their comments and thoughts, as well as being a model of an epic marriage.

Special thanks to my daughter Aleah, for the time spent reading and editing the manuscript and sharing her thoughts.

Thanks to Nellie Keasling for her editorial gifts.

Special thanks to my friend and graphic art designer Lonna Gattenby for her inspiring the design.

And last, but not least, special thanks to Jenny, my loving wife, for coauthoring this book with me. Your views and sage insights have made the book more balanced and inclusive. Your partnership in doing this project has been invaluable, as you allowed the Holy Spirit to unearth and utilize your gifting to collaboratively work to produce a book that glorifies God.

We give tribute to all who offered suggestions, insights, and prayers. So, if reading this book impacts one or 1 million lives, your help will have been rewarded.

Finally, we thank God for choosing us as instruments to pen these words. To Him be all the glory. Without Him this book would not have been possible.

INTRODUCTION

It's God's intention for all human beings to live epic lives. Adam and Eve, the first married couple, was made to have an epic relationship. They did live an epic life for a short time until sin marred it.

To live in an average or mediocre marital relationship is a choice. Likewise, epic relationship is also a choice. Neither an average, mediocre, or epic relationship happens by chance. The amount of time, energy, and commitment couples invest in their relationships will determine the quality, or lack thereof, of their marital outcome. As married couples, we make our lives what it is. If you are not happy with the state of your marriage, *you* have the power and resources at your fingertips to change it if you want. Not the single you, but the plural you.

You see, the beauty of a plant is not determined by how it was planted, but by how well it was cared for after it was planted. Likewise, the quality of a marriage is not measured by how it began, but by how it is nurtured and sustained.

A farmer must take time to cultivate and care for the plant; otherwise, it might die. The same thing is true with a piano or baseball player. Someone could be given a piano or baseball, they could learn some skills about each instrument, but if they do not practice daily and care for their equipment, they will not become a Mozart or Michael Jordan. The more love, time, and energy couples consistently invest in their relationships, the healthier their marriages will become.

According to Rabbi Yitzchak Ginsburgh, in his article, "Love at First Sight: Five Biblical Examples," "When God created Eve and presented her to Adam, Adam exclaimed: "This time, bone of my bones and flesh of my flesh! This one shall be called 'woman,' for she was taken from man" (Genesis 2:23). By saying spontaneously, "This time," he expressed his delight and emotional arousal—his love at first sight—for his newfound mate."[1]

This was Adam's first verbal response when his eyes beheld his beautiful partner and wife. Not all relationships began at the first sight like Adam, Rachel, and Rebekah. But, all loving relationships require certain elements to grow into the epic marriage that God wants. This is what this book is about. If you want to be the epic, wholehearted lover you were created to be, open your heart and your relationship to become what you were created to be.

God created marital relationships to live in wonder, punctuated with some great events and rites. According to the Genesis account of creation, Moses tells us that human beings were made differently from animals, birds, sea creatures, and creeping things to display the prominent standards of legendary heroes of God's creation. God formed the first couple and placed them in the epicenter of His creation—the Garden of Eden. From that center they were to live lives of love, have children, repopulate the world, and set up a kingdom of loving beings.

Humans were God's masterpiece, and their relationships were created to replicate God's ideals. Human relationships were not designed to model off great lovers in literature like *Romeo and Juliet*, *Gone With the Wind*, *Wuthering Heights*, or *Titanic*. Neither was it designed to model off the characters of Solomon and Shulamite, Abraham and Sarah, or Jacob and Rebekah, as wonderful as these marriages were.

Introduction

All the aforementioned relationships were great love stories, and they all had some resemblance of epic marriages. But the only place we can go to find a true model of epic marriage, is in the creation narrative of Adam and Eve.

Usually, when a reader looks for an epic love story, one generally looks for some special characteristics as outlined by literary scholars. Literary scholars contend that to call a story epic, the character needs to have a "bigger than life narrative." The narrative should be set within a metanarrative. The character needs to exemplify valor, deeds, bravery, charisma, and personality. They look for a person, who has incredible physical and mental traits. They are great exaggerations to make an impression on the audience. The character is helped by a supernatural power, influencing morality by which the narrative is developed. The theme of each epic is sublime, elegant, and has universal significance. It impacts a metanarrative. Finally, the language of every epic story is lofty, grand, and elegant. Jenny and I believe that was the life God wanted for all marital relationships, beginning with Adam and Eve's marriage.

Adam and Eve's sins shortchanged that purpose, but it did not stop or change God's desire to make marriage relationships epic. He has made a way to restore that goal through the second Adam, Jesus Christ. Thank God for the second chance. Your marriage might not be epic now, but the God of second chances is ready and waiting to transform your average marriage into the epic marriage it was created to be.

To understand the word "epic," it is imperative to know the etymology of the word *epic*. The word *epic* is derived from a Greek word *epikos*, which means "a word, song, or speech." According to *Webster's New World Dictionary, epic* "is a long narrative poem in a dignified style about the deeds of a traditional or historical hero or heroes. An epic is a long narrative in verse."

The problem with many marriage relationships is, they are stuck in the sinful model of the fallen couple, rather than choosing to pursue the epic model.

This volume is committed to leading its readers to regain the epic status for their marriage as God intends. So, begin today to say like Gianna Jessen (an abortion survivor) said in an article written by Rachel del Guidice, "Average Love or Epic Love."

> I don't want average love. I want the epic love story. If people waited for God, He would do more than you could believe.

Guidice further says, epic exists.

> If people wait for God, He would do more than you could believe. God is the author of life. He is the author of love. What better person could there possibly be to write your love story?[2]

Epic love begins with who is in control of the marriage.

As we unfold the elements of epic love, couples must learn to relinquish their wants, desires, timetables, and stipulations and acknowledge God's sovereign power over the marriage. Couples need to build their marriage on the right foundation, embrace right communication and conflict management skills. They need to invest time, talent, and all their resources to learn in the discipleship love lab. Learning to love is the most important thing epic marriages are made of and, contrary to popular culture, our love lives are our own invention.

Having created Adam and Eve with all the rights elements for an epic marriage, God blessed them and sent them to go and, "be fruitful." Go practice love, pure love. He

Introduction

did not say go be a martyr or a codependent lover. He said go be a real lover.

Epic marriages are made of empowered participants investing compassionately in their relationships. Marriage was created to require work. No superstar earned superstardom by wishing, dreaming, or praying. They reached and sustained that status by working and practicing their skills systemically and regularly with devotions and dedication. They worked at their trades through all the stages of life. Likewise, epic married couples allow the Holy Spirit to guide them through all the stages of marriage to remain faithful and epic lovers.

Finally, in closing this introduction, we want to highlight one of the main characteristics of epic couples, which is, they always want to communicate their comprehension with other like-minded couples. Therefore, we have decided to end each chapter with a few review questions. These questions are optional. However, we feel one sure way to know if you have gained sufficient information to build your marriage and help other couples is by answering the questions correctly. If you would like to verify the correctness of your answers, please wait until you have read and answered all the questions in the chapters, then go to pp. 235-244 where an answer sheet is provided.

—Dr. Daniel and Jenny Vassell

End Notes

[1] https://www.chabad.org/library/article_cdo/aid/3176/jewish/Love-at-First-Sight-Five-Biblical-Examples.htm

[2] https://chastityproject.com/2014/10/average-love-epic-love/

CHAPTER 1

EPIC LOVERS' MARRIAGE

One of the major fallacies many couples believed for their marriage is the notion that if they created the best proposals, engagements, and/or wedding celebrations, they would have laid a solid marital foundation, thereby guaranteeing a successful married life. Oh, if that were only true, we would have some of the most healthy and wealthy people living in our world today. The lessons from history tell us that misconception is not true.

Over 1 billion people watched the epic fairytale wedding of Princess Diana and Prince Charles, and then later watched the separation, divorce, and death of Princess Diana. No doubt many of you who are reading this book can recall family members, friends, and loved ones who had wonderful, creative, and amazing weddings plans that left you spellbound, but only to later see these marriages end up in separation and divorce. After these epic beginnings, one wonders how could that be? There are untold stories of millions of couples who entered and created epic marriages only to end up later in separation and divorce. Increasingly, this is becoming the norm instead of the exception in our postmodern context.

These epic marriages began with lavish weddings that create romantic ambiances and memories to last a lifetime. It illustrated their mutual love and created precious memories they wished to leave in the hearts of their families and friends. However, all epic marriages may not have the stars and sparkles at the beginning of their journey; but with the right attitude, knowledge, skills, tools, and experience, coupled with the grace and wisdom of God, they will be able to successfully navigate the choppy marital waters of life into an epic marriage.

I wrote the first *Love Factor in Marriage* book in the '90s, when one of the vexing issues plaguing marriages at that time was the high divorce rates. During this era, it was commonly reported that marriages, particularly Christian marriages, were in deep trouble. However, it was later proven that such findings were distorted and lacking in credibility.

Ed Stetzer, president of Lifeway Research Center, sets the record straight in an article titled, *Pastors: That Divorce Stat You Quoted Is Probably Wrong*, when he said, "People who seriously practice a traditional religious faith—whether Christian or other—have a divorce rate markedly lower than the general population." That's good news, but it is not the end. Stetzer continues,

> *...all epic marriages may not have the stars and sparkles at the beginning of their journey; but with the right attitude, knowledge, skills, tools, and experience, coupled with the grace and wisdom of God...*

> The factor making the most difference is religious commitment and practice. ... Couples who regularly practice any combination of serious religious behaviors and attitudes—attend church nearly

every week; read their Bibles and spiritual materials regularly; pray privately and together; generally, take their faith seriously, living not as perfect disciples but serious disciples—enjoy significantly lower divorce rates than mere church members, the general public, and unbelievers.[1]

This is good news for Christian couples who are experiencing the epic marriage God ordains. It is not the lavishness at the beginning of marriage that is important for epic Christian marriages, it is having the right ingredients to create them.

Couples in epic marriages are committed to their religious practices such as attending church regularly. They are very committed to reading their Bibles and maintaining devoted prayer lives.

Some may ask: What is an epic marriage? For right now, let us say that an *epic marriage*

> ... is an extremely awesome relationship. It is a marriage that seeks to show forth the glory of God, in good times and not so good times. It is a marriage that does not seek self-happiness, but other-happiness. It experiences growth through the plethora of struggles and challenges it encounters in marriage. It is a marriage in which couples acquire the requisite skills, tools, and knowledge to effectively manage and overcome their marital adversaries, conquer struggles, and experience the transformation deemed necessary to become better persons.

An epic married couple demonstrates humble hearts governed by love, executes deeds to exemplify and glorify God, and personifies godly standards that are esteemed by the Word of God, empowered by the Spirit of God, and revered by the Spirit-filled community of faith.

Epic marriages are valued within society and most couples marry with the intention of having an epic relationship. The major challenge in Christian marriage is no longer divorce if "epic couples" continue to engage in spiritual practices, according to Stetzer. One of the great challenges that epic Christian marriages face today is the redefinition of biblical marriage by the political authorities.

Many countries in the West have surrendered to the gay lobby and have chosen to accept the "new normal," where morality is no longer based on absolutes but on relativism. It is a new morality which is based on rights not absolutes. In other words, "it does not matter whom you love, as long as you are not hurting anyone; if it feels so good, it can't be wrong." This argument suggests that there is a significant cultural shift in marriage from the traditional biblical view of "one man to one woman." By abandoning the Judeo-Christian ethic concerning marriage, we are opening the door for the perversion of marriage as designed by God.

> "It is a marriage in which couples acquire the requisite skills, tools, and knowledge to effectively manage and overcome their marital adversaries, conquer struggles, and experience the transformation deemed necessary to become better persons."

Increasingly, marriage is becoming one of the most politically charged and discussed issues in our postmodern culture. In this milieu, it is promoted, celebrated, and embraced as a good thing to pursue. However, the challenge is people want to change the biblical or Judeo-Christian definition of one man, one woman marriage, replaced by a more sanitized, relativized, inoffensive, inclusive version, which says you can marry whomever you want, with the only criteria being "love." In others words, it does not matter whom you love. However, the epic marriage is erected on the biblical model "one man and one woman," to the exclusion of all others.

Gary Thomas, in his book, *Sacred Marriage*, says,

> Marriage is more than a sacred covenant with another person. It is a spiritual discipline designed to help you know God better, trust him more fully, and love him more deeply.[2]

Hence, the highest purpose of love in an epic marriage is to serve and care for each other in ways that reveal the glory of God in the union.

Epic marriage was created to work in a partnership of one husband, one wife, empowered by the Holy Spirit—a holy triad. It is believed that was the reason God carefully chose where the surgery was performed on Adam to source Eve. God took a rib from the side of Adam. Students of the Word believe the Hebrew word for "rib can also mean "side." The selection of the word, says it clearly that she was created to be in partnership, side by side.

She was given as a supporting partner, a helpmeet. She was not a subordinate or inferior partner, but she was given to be a helpmeet as God was to Moses as recorded in Exodus 18:4. This marriage arrangement was holy because God made it and set it apart for Himself, serving as the third person in the relationship. I, Daniel, would like to add here that marital success does not occur because the Holy Spirit is a resident in the marriage. The success does not rest so much on the relationship dynamics between the couple, but on the couple's yielding to the Holy Spirit and making Him "president" of the relationship.

When the Holy Spirit is allowed to be in charge, the marriage and family live in joy and thankfulness (Ephesians 5:18-20). When the Holy Spirit is leading the marriage and family, husbands and wives will submit to each other (Ephesians 5:21).

The wife will submit to her husband's loving and caring leadership (Ephesians 5:22-24). The husband will submit to God's commands of loving his wife sacrificially, while cherishing and nourishing her (Ephesians 5:25-32).

Many Christian couples consider the Ephesians 5 narrative as only a recommendation and not a motif for an epic marriage. But the truth is, it is not a recommendation. It is a model and description of epic marriages yielding to the Holy Spirit. With the Holy Spirit being the leading third person, the mystery of marriage will be revealed. Ephesians 5:32 tells us epic marriage demonstrates and reveals the loving union that is modeled by Christ and the Church. That kind of epic union is only possible with the aid of the Holy Spirit.

> *The success of Spirit-filled Christian marriages cannot be equated to romantic love and feelings. Romantic love and feelings at the basic level is often conditional, sporadic, temporary, and transitional. Instead, epic Spirit–filled marriages are built on prayer, compassion, and the infilling of the Holy Spirit.*

The success of Spirit-filled Christian marriages cannot be equated to romantic love and feelings. Romantic love and feelings at the basic level is often conditional, sporadic, temporary, and transitional. Instead, epic Spirit–filled marriages are built on prayer, compassion, and the infilling of the Holy Spirit.

The Holy Spirit infilling comes through prayer. He enables couples to love each other unconditionally, demonstrating the willingness to serve each other's needs through compassion. Epic lovers do not rely so much on counselors, therapists, books, and other external resources to help them build their marriages and families or resolve marital and family problems. Instead, they first seek the Holy Spirit's help through prayer. Epic couples know that when they pray, they open their hearts to God and invite the Holy Spirit to release healing to resolve marital issues.

There are four main ingredients in an epic marriage. They are: empowerment, prayer, investment, and compassion. All four ingredients must be actively employed in the marital union at the same time, although they might not necessarily be operating at the same levels. The order in which we will explore each ingredient is the following: prayer, empowerment, investment, and compassion. However, we created an acrostic for the word "EPIC" to help us grasp, understand, and remember these truths a little easier:

E – Empowered, Spirit-living Encourager
P – Partner-focused petitionary prayer (PFPP)
I – Intimate investor
C – Compassionate caregiver

Let us begin with the element of partner-focused petitionary prayer's influence in marriage.

Partner-focused Petitionary Prayer (PFPP)

Do not think for a moment that EPIC marriages and families are straightjacket Christians who do not have fun in their marriage. They do! They experience emotional bonds, romantic escapades, and marital thrills just like every other Christian. However, the vitality for epic marriages and families is not anchored on feelings, but in the quality of time that couples and families spend in prayer.

When the nostalgic feelings of marriage are low and the stresses and struggles of reality are high, there is the temptation to throw in the towel and run away and hide. Where should epic couples turn for help and comfort when these feelings occur? They should turn to God in prayer.

Couples know that neither one in their marriage is perfect. Sometimes our mates act perfectly and sometimes they do not; and during the not so perfect times, the challenges seem to overwhelm us. The best way to deal with those moments of imperfection is to engage the weapon of prayer. The not so perfect times have the potential to engender and incubate hurtful feelings that could make the not so perfect time become a disastrous experience. What is a good way out or through these times? The epic couples call on God in prayer.

For a long time, there were ideological camps that would call this approach a copout. Studies are now providing evidence of the impact of prayer in marital relationships. According to a new study coauthored by Frank D. Fincham, eminent scholar and director of the Florida State University Family Institute (FSU), "Praying for a romantic partner or close friend can lead to more cooperative and forgiving behavior toward the partner."[3] This is a remarkable finding because the report comes from the partners who were the subject of the prayers, and they reported a positive change in the behavior of the person who prayed.

> "My previous research had shown that those who prayed for their partner reported more prosocial behavior toward their partner," Fincham argues. "This set of studies is the very first to use objective indicators to show that prayer changed actual behavior and that this behavior was apparent to the other partner, the subject of the prayer."[4]

Fincham is one of several authors of the study led by Nathanial Lambert, a former FSU doctoral student who is now an assistant professor at Brigham Young University. Their paper, "Shifting Toward Cooperative Tendencies and Forgiveness: How Partner-Focused Prayer Transforms Motivation," was published in the journal *Personal Relationships*. In addition to Lambert and Fincham, the coauthors are C. Nathan DeWall and Richard Pond of the University of Kentucky, and Steven R. Beach of the University of Georgia.

The paper cites the results of five separate studies designed to find out whether partner-focused prayer shifts individuals toward cooperative behaviors and tendencies both over time and in the immediate aftermath of hurtful behavior.

These are among the findings:

1. Participants who prayed more frequently for their partner were rated as less vengeful in discussing something the partner had done to upset or annoy them.
2. The partners of participants who prayed for them noticed more forgiving behavior than the partners of participants who were assigned to set aside time each day to think positive thoughts about them.
3. Participants assigned to pray after a partner's hurtful behavior were more cooperative with their partners compared to participants assigned to engage in thinking about God.
4. Participants who prayed for a close-relationship partner on days in which conflict occurred reported higher levels of cooperative tendencies and forgiveness than on days when conflict occurred, and they did not pray. (Source: *Charisma News: Faith and Family*).[5]

Doug Small, in one of his books on prayer, says,

> The absence of prayer in the home is more damaging than its absence in the church; in fact, when prayer is something strange and foreign to daily life, we create something very different from New Testament Christianity.[6]

We create something dissimilar to the traditional Spirit-led family paradigm as well.

A University of Chicago survey revealed that 75 percent of Americans who pray with their spouses report their marriages are, "very happy." Those who prayed together were more likely to respect each other, discuss their marriage goals together, and, in a surprising find for the University, reported high levels of satisfaction in the area of couple intimacy.[7]

> *Prayer should not be a chore or a burden. It should be entered at the appropriate times that will suit each family's schedule. God is more interested that we come to Him in prayer daily than becoming slaves to a prayer time.*

The cure for most of our marital and family ills will take place when the family altar is restored to a place of primacy in our Christian homes and communities. Many families, as well as couples, are receiving help from books and other resources; but without the indispensable ingredient of prayer, their journey becomes more difficult.

There are many benefits to be derived when prayer is incorporated into the daily lives of marriage and family. The family as a unit, as well as each member, is endued with supernatural power to cope with the challenges of personal and family life. New data reveals that when couples receive premarital counseling and pray together, the probability of divorce is one in 39,000.[8] This report tells us, when couples pray together, the probability of divorce is significantly diminished.

As a word of encouragement to our Spirit-led church, if we are hoping to stem the tide of divorce, we must not only provide enrichment seminars, workshops, retreats, books, and other resources, but we must also encourage couples and families to rebuild their family altars. According to Small,

> Every husband and wife should pray together daily if possible, and not less than weekly. A cup of coffee in the morning combined with a morning prayer is a good way to begin the day. Add a devotional: Read Scripture together. Read through the Bible together in a year. Select a book to study together. Pray together regularly for your children and grandchildren. Call them by name. Pause over each name and give the Holy Spirit an opportunity to impress your heart and mind.[9]

As I, Daniel, reflect on my family of origin, I can testify today that it was the family altar that kept my parents together. It was those early morning family prayers that kept our family together in some of the most difficult times. I must confess that as a child, I resented early morning prayers. It was not that I did not like to pray, it was just done too early in the morning. At 5:00 a.m., all I wanted to do was sleep, but for my father, that was prayer time.

Prayer has helped us navigate the challenging times and kept our marriage and family together in both the good and bad times. It was through prayer that we were able to cover our children under the mighty hand of God and lead them through the various stages of their development, still loving God and the church. Today, they are pursuing the will of God for their own lives. The only difference with my family's prayer time and my parents' is, when my children lived with us, we did not pray at 5:00 a.m. Sometimes, we prayed in the mornings at breakfast or before we went to bed. We were committed to daily prayer, but we were flexible with the times of day.

There are many who advocate a set time for daily prayers. It is difficult in our complicated and busy lives to find rigid times for prayer. Prayer should not be a chore or a burden. It should be entered at the appropriate times that will suit each family's schedule. God is more interested that we come to Him in prayer daily than becoming slaves to a prayer time. As Spirit-led Christians, we must return to praying together as couples and family. God wants to meet our marital and family needs. The Bible tells us, "Where two or three are gathered, He is in the midst" (see Matthew 18:20). He is in the midst to meet our needs.

Doug Small told a few stories of how prayer made a difference in couples' lives, and I think they will encourage you. One of them was about a couple named Liz and Tom. He told the story of a loveless marriage that was dark and in serious trouble. "Alcohol had come in," Liz said. Tom added that bringing the Lord into their lives and praying together saved the marriage.

> Doug and Beth's marriage was in trouble. Three children, two job changes, and two 1,000-mile moves had stressed the relationship to the breaking point. Beth, in a bold attempt to save the relationship, asked her husband, Doug, to begin praying with her. Doug was not a Christian. In fact, he was nonreligious, a self-proclaimed man of science. But Doug felt that if saying prayers with Beth could save the relationship, it was worth a try.
>
> "I soon found that praying together brings out a real sense of selflessness and humility. When you're praying for each other, not just yourself, you're focused together and speaking from the heart on a whole different level. I would never have predicted this for us, but it really works," said Doug.

"As bad as any problem may seem at that moment," agrees Beth, "prayer always helps us see beyond it. It doesn't have to be a long-drawn-out Scripture reading, just a few minutes a day. When we pray, it brings another level of honesty to our conversations. I think it's the most intimate thing you can do with another person."[10]

Now they pray together every night. When couples and families pray together, they are modeling the example Christ set in prayer.

Prayer provides a safe and regular forum in which couples invite God into their personal and marital struggles. It also provides opportunity for your mate to hear your concerns, especially spiritual and relational ones. They develop a capacity for greater openness with one another, which enables them to minister to each other's concerns with a view of resolving their issues.

Prayer builds a bond between couples that makes them stronger—I'm not talking about the physical attraction toward each other, but a more emotional and spiritual bond that increases the likelihood of unity in the relationship. They will discover that they consistently share similar issues and concerns. They invite God to intervene in their lives and in the lives of their children. And He does.

Couples who pray about their family, business concerns, finances, marital issues, and giving to the Kingdom and God's work, report miraculous results from prayer. The number of disagreements declines. Couples are taking their stresses to God in prayer, looking to Him for answers. As a result, they tend to be more patient with each other and see things from an eternal perspective. Praying together lays a spiritual foundation for a spiritual legacy for their children.

Epic couples commit themselves to making prayer one of the main elements of their marriage. They realize that the only way they can overcome spiritual attacks against their marriage is to rely on God through prayer. When epic couples pray, the Spirit of God destroys and overcomes spiritual attacks. When they pray, the Spirit of God furnishes the wisdom and knowledge to love their mate through the life changes in marriage and family. Many people see epic couples and families and wish to have their kind of life. It is not that epic couples do not have serious problems in their marriage and family; it's that they commit themselves to God through prayer, and He empowers them for the journey.

Prayer provides a safe and regular forum in which couples invite God into their personal and marital struggles.

Prayer Goals for Couples

Beyond praying for each other and the needs of family and home, Doug Small enumerated a helpful list in his book, which, if adopted in couples' prayer lives, will prove to be immensely beneficial in the end.

- Pray daily for your children.
- Pray for unsaved family members and friends, work associates, and neighbors.
- Designate at least one day a week or month to pray for your pastor and other spiritual leaders.
- Pray regularly for a church ministry.
- Adopt at least one missionary for prayer. If you can't send financial support, pray for them.
- Adopt an unreached people group. Make it your prayer project. Pray until you hear that God has raised up a missionary to go and reach them, then pray for the missionary.

- Adopt a parachurch ministry for prayer—one that works with local schools, the homeless, unwed mothers, seniors, or unity causes in the community.
- Pray for political leaders. Choose a mayor, a city council person, a state legislator, a national legislator, the president, or a member of his staff. Send the person you choose a note, saying, "I'm praying for you."
- Create a couple's prayer triad with two other couples. Adopt mutual projects for prayer. Confer with one another monthly. Share information about the people, ministries, and causes you are praying about. Get together once a quarter for an evening of prayer and sharing. Pray for one another's kids.
- Pray for others, particularly for the Kingdom purposes of God. Be missional in your praying.
- Pray with a vision for harvest.[11]

As you were reading, hopefully, you have noticed that we have spent much time sharing on the subject of prayer. It was intentional and necessary. Someone may ask: Why do we spend so much time on prayer? Many of the issues couples and families share with counselors and therapists could be better resolved at the family altar through prayer. However, we must lay down one important caveat; that is, prayer is not the only means Spirit-led couples employ in dealing with marriage and family issues.

There is still the need to get professional help with issues that praying alone does not resolve. There may be some marital issues and challenges that God might want couples and families to seek counseling or therapy for, but He will provide the grace for you to grow more like Him through that integrative, therapeutic process. Counselors and therapists are servants of the Lord, but they must be consulted with and through prayer.

Epic couples will always encounter problems in their marriages, but they can find help from the Creator of marriage through prayer. It was in prayer the early church received power to become bold witnesses for Christ. It is through the medium of prayer Spirit-filled couples, being witnesses of Christ, are able to demonstrate to the world the glory of God. When couples and families pray together, they are tapping into an inexhaustible supply of resources made available to them by the Holy Spirit for their daily living.

Empowered, Spirit-living Encourager

Epic couples and families are Spirit-empowered believers because they commit their lives, marriages, and families to the Lord. The strength and stability of their relationships are sourced in the Word of God. Hence, they refuse to be influenced by the *zeitgeist*—the secular cultural norms concerning marriage. Instead, they read, study, and meditate on the Word; depending on the Word of God to guide them through the contorted maze of the postmodern age.

Epic couples look for sound marital principles enshrined in the Word of God from which to pattern and build their relationships. One such passage is Ephesians 5:18–6:1-5. In this passage, the apostle Paul declared that an epic marriage which will glorify God must begin with the empowerment of the Holy Spirit. Listen to what he said to the Ephesians: "Stop getting drunk with wine, which leads to wild living, but keep on being filled with the Spirit" (5:18 ISV). In this text, Paul tells the Ephesian church to be filled with the Holy Spirit; otherwise, the wrong spirit will lead to wild living. On the contrary, he called for the church to be filled with a continuous infilling of the Holy Spirit.

Here, it is important to note that Paul was not advocating the total abstinence of wine nor was he advocating the drinking of wine. Paul knew that wine has great medicinal values, so he was not condemning drinking it.

He did admonish Timothy to drink some wine for his "stomach's sake" (see 1 Timothy 5:23). Contextually, a thorough examination of text would reveal that both wine and the infilling of the Spirit are good when they are used and placed in the right order. Here Paul was admonishing the church, especially married couples, to seek the infilling of the Holy Spirit. Why?

Note that implicit in Paul's argument is the notion that the overindulgence of wine (a good thing) will lead to intoxication and ultimately to wild and uncontrolled living. The application here is, the overuse of any "good thing" in a marriage can replace or substitute the role of the Holy Spirit in a marriage. These "good things" tend to lead to problems which will eventually replace or remove primacy of the Holy Spirit.

> *Epic couples will always encounter problems in their marriages, but they can find help from the Creator of marriage through prayer.*

Right now, you may know of couples or families who are being held together by the wrong wine/spirit/third person. It could be their work, children, hobbies and interests, sports, in-laws, friends, church activities, money, etc. When these interests take over and replace the Holy Spirit in couples and families' lives, they become empty, and they look for an escape. Escape is not the answer! A refilling of the right Spirit is.

Today, many marriages and families are hurting because they are living under the influence of the wrong spirit that is leading them into wild marital or family relationships. They have allowed the wrong third person inside to take them through their marriage. They didn't do it on purpose, of course! It just happened. That is the result of not actively protecting their marriages by praying and allowing the Holy Spirit the opportunity to lead.

There are many things in the world that compete for our love. Sometimes, these forces are so strong that they diminish our relationships with our mates. Many couples have allowed some good things to replace the infilling of the Holy Spirit; therefore, what is holding their unions together is not the right Spirit. It was not their intention to allow these good things to lead them astray.

What are some of the possible reasons why these third persons (wines) enter marriages and families? It is believed that a third person happens as a natural consequence of intimacy. Not knowing one's limits, the person spends too much time on individual projects, taking the marriage for granted and ignoring marital needs. They have problems in setting boundaries with others—they cannot separate from friends or family. Couples have an inability to live with differences—politics, food, and traditional likes and dislikes. The pressures, temptations, and even genuinely good opportunities coming from the outside world are limitless. As stewards of the marriage covenant, epic lovers know how to structure their relationship so that the outside doesn't control what is inside.

The apostle Paul was fully aware that the devil would like to counterfeit God's wine for marriage. So, he challenged couples to desist from allowing wine to control their lives, instead they should daily seek the empowerment wine of the Holy Spirit.

Currently, a vast number of couples and families are living in a state of unhappiness. But Paul continued by sharing with us that when believers are filled with the Spirit, they will be happy with themselves and with God. As happy individuals or couples, they will "recite to one another psalms, hymns, and spiritual songs. You will sing and make music to the Lord with your hearts" (Ephesians 5: 19 ISV). He further stated that couples and families will develop an attitude of gratitude, contentment with themselves, mates, family, and others (Ephesians 5:20).

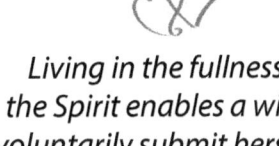

Living in the fullness of the Spirit enables a wife to voluntarily submit herself to the loving leadership of her husband (Ephesians 5:22-24). Living in the fullness of the Spirit also allows husbands to love their wives with unconditional commitment.

When couples are filled with the Holy Spirit they live in a loving and harmonious marriage relationship where there is mutual submission, as stated in Ephesians 5:21. The Holy Spirit prompts a mutual attitude of respect for each other, enabling couples to operate as partners in their relationship. In this milieu, the partners will use their gifts for the holistic benefits of the marriage and not for themselves.

Living in the fullness of the Spirit enables a wife to voluntarily submit herself to the loving leadership of her husband (Ephesians 5:22-24). Living in the fullness of the Spirit also allows husbands to love their wives with unconditional commitment. The Holy Spirit will lead husbands to meet the needs of their wives, even if this means "giving up their lives," just as Christ sacrificed His life for the Church. Yes, a Spirit-filled husband will treat his wife with the same love and respect he has for himself (Ephesians 5:25–33). Without the empowerment of the Holy Spirit as the third person in the marriage, the marriage will be on shaky ground. Without His involvement in the marriage, it will not operate to its maximum and will be devoid of the richness and quality of love deemed necessary for an EPIC marriage.

Intimate Investor

So much is written about the necessity of love in marriage, but much more is needed. Why? You may ask. The answer is simple. The topic is limitless, and no one author can exhaust its height, depth, and breadth. When couples and families are living with the Spirit's empowerment, it is very easy to love. Epic couples invest time to show love to their spouse and family. True love does not come easily without the Holy Spirit's help. Showing unconditional love requires a willingness to invest time, money, energy, and patience. Epic couples do not base their love upon conditional love only. You may ask, Why? The answer is: *Eros* love needs the right condition, atmosphere, and attitude to share it. *Phileo* love needs the right friendship to share it. *Storge* love needs the right bonding to express it. *Epithumia* love may need the right look, touch, words, smell, and feeling to fulfill; on the other hand, unconditional love requires a willingness to invest actions without feelings.

It is very easy to love when all the feelings are right. On the other hand, it is very difficult to share unconditional love when there is no internal or external motivation. Unconditional love requires an investment that is motivated by the mind to choose to act differently, even when the feeling is contrary. It requires actions that cause hurtful feelings. A careful reading of the Hosea narrative in chapter 3, verse 1 tells us that God told Hosea to "go again" and love Gomer. We believe Hosea did not have any more loving feelings for

Gomer. Hence, God told him to go and love her with His love—unconditional love.

Epic lovers are committed to invest in their marriage and families even when it does not feel right. They are willing to give all and spend all for the greater good of their union and marriage. When that kind of love is invested, it has the potential to reap rich dividends. We are reminded in the Word of God that "love covers a multitude of sins" (1 Peter 4:8 ISV). This is not only true spiritually, but it is also true in a marital context. Paul tells us that Jesus invested His love in order to redeem the church, thereby cleansing her of all her sins, presenting her blameless, without blemish, etc. (Ephesians 5:28-30).

The story of Hosea tells of one who was willing to invest in his marriage and family to create an Epic relationship. It was not easy, but he recommitted himself and invested in the marriage. He knew that his marriage would only be as strong as what it cost to provide, protect, and preserve it. In other words, Hosea valued what he invested in. If you have spent time, effort, and sacrifice in preserving your marriage from other influences, the odds of an epic husband and wife marriage will be seen.

We were told that Hosea married Gomer, a prostitute, and had children (Hosea 1). She became unfaithful in the marriage and left him to go back to a life of prostitution (Hosea 2). After she left him as a single parent, he took care of the children (Hosea 3:1). "Go yet," seemed to imply that Hosea went several times to try to reconcile his marriage, but to no avail. However, God instructed him to go again and

It is very easy to love when all the feelings are right. On the other hand, it is very difficult to share unconditional love when there is no internal or external motivation.

love unconditionally his "unfaithful wife." These were not "feelings" of love such as *philio, storage, Eros,* or *epithumia*, but an unconditional love. She did not deserve it, but she needed it if she were ever going to be saved, healed, and delivered.

Hosea had to invest money—15 shekels of silver and 1.5 homers of barley—to buy back his own wife (Hosea 3:2). He invested time. "It will take time for healing and creating a new and holy habit." He invested patience to wait until she was sexually delivered before he became intimate with her again.

Epic lovers are committed to spend all, to give all, so that they can gain all. Why motivate epic lovers to invest in their marriage and family? They realize that love is not only needed for marriage in the *here* and *now*, but also it will transcend time (1 Corinthians 13:13). So, Epic lovers commit to practicing love in their marriage and family, because it's the truest remedy for life and eternity.

The kind of unconditional love that is needed in marriage can only be fully experienced with the aid of the Holy Spirit. No natural man or woman can love perfectly without help from the God of love—the Holy Spirit. To be able to fulfill and maintain the loving actions and thought processes required in marriage and families, one would need to be an angel, or a person constantly being filled with the Spirit.

When we look at some of the love commands for Christians found in Scripture, such as outlined in Galatians 5:22-23 and 1 Corinthians 13:1, we know that we need the help of the Holy Spirit to love through us.

When couples and families live with the continuous infilling and refilling of the Holy Spirit, husbands will be empowered to truly love their wives unconditionally, even when they may not deserve it. Likewise, wives will truly respect their husbands unconditionally, even when their actions suggest otherwise. Only the empowerment of the Holy Spirit can help couples fulfill Ephesians 5:33, "…each individual man among you must (unconditionally) love his wife as he loves himself; and may the wife (unconditionally) fear (respect) her husband" (ISV).

The apostle Paul outlined a rich description of the kind of love that should be in Christian marriages and families. This kind of love mentioned in 1 Corinthians 13 is beyond human comprehension and it is impossible to exercise daily in marriage and family, without the indwelling presence of the Holy Spirit. It is only when couples are truly living in the Spirit that they are empowered to operate in the fruit of love (Galatians 5:22-23).

> *Epic lovers are committed to spend all, to give all, so that they can gain all.*

Christian marriages and families need the love of Galatians 5:22-23 to assist them in the daily grind of marriage and family stresses. How can mere human beings love as 1 Corinthians 13 commands? In my opinion, it is not humanly possible, but with the empowerment released in us by the infilling of the Holy Spirit, we will be able to graciously demonstrate the loving traits and actions required for an epic marriage and family.

Compassionate Caregiver/Acts of Kindness

One of the greatest challenges in 21st-century marriages and families is the individual thinking and behavior patterns. It is sad when you see many married couples living as if they are still single. Epic couples do not live for their own selfish desires; instead, they're moved with compassion to serve each other in love. They live to do acts of kindness for their mates and families. They live in a caregiving mode.

There are two schools of thought that motivate the spirit of compassion, leading to acts of kindness. One is, "loving feelings lead to loving actions." The other view is, "loving actions lead to loving feelings." The answers to both schools of thought are, yes. Both schools are correct, in the sense that one is not preferred to the exclusion of the other. In marriage and family, both are utilized because of compassion.

Compassion is easily released when couples are experiencing loving feelings toward each other. Their brains are flooded with dopamine, endorphins, serotonin, and other chemicals, which lead them to perform acts of kindness. But if epic lovers were to depend on loving feelings alone to lead to loving actions at all times, this would be catastrophic.

We cannot depend on feelings alone, because they are often temporary and fleeting; simply put, our feelings have the propensity to betray or lead us astray. Many epic couples would not survive the challenges of marriage.

If epic marriages depended on feelings only, the devil would have a heyday in marriage and families. He would unleash his emissaries, demons, and fallen angels to release all kinds of challenges to sabotage the health and well-being of marriage and family. Epic lovers are caregivers committed to a compassion that moves them to a higher spiritual level of service. They move in compassion by putting themselves in the shoes of their mate or family to identify with their hurt, then choose to take on the infirmity and serve with loving actions to soothe and heal the pain.

> *We cannot depend on feelings alone, because they are often temporary and fleeting; simply put, our feelings have the propensity to betray or lead us astray.*

Besides the evil spiritual forces attacking marriage and family, there are many other unresolved childhood and adult traumas causing pain and hurt; epic lovers need compassion to stand in the gap and provide a safe place for their healing and restoration. Epic lovers empathize with each other. They do not condemn; they offer comfort and solace. When a mate hits rock bottom in the marriage or family, it is here that the spouse is called upon to offer loving action that isn't motivated by loving feelings. It is here through daily prayer, that their bond and intimacy increase with the enablement of the Holy Spirit. The Holy Spirit ignites and releases a desire to serve each other, where they are able to meet each other's needs, thereby minimizing self-loathing caused by pain and hurt.

In our Western world, most marriages begin with chemically induced, loving feelings, while in the Eastern culture, it begins with a commitment and involuntary actions to where loving feelings follow. In whatever way a marriage begins, we know that as time progresses, the routine and mundane responsibilities of daily living have a tendency to reduce the nostalgic feelings, which if unchecked, tend to lead to lack of love and affection. Many couples have depended on only their loving feelings to lead them in marriage for too long. If you are one who finds you are operating only in a loving feeling mode and your marriage and family are on the rocks, invite your family to the altar. Call on the Lord of marriage, and I assure you, the Holy Spirit will enter and restore what is needed. Your wrong feelings have been producing the wrong results in your marriage and family.

When epic couples share together in prayer, they open the doors of their hearts to the Holy Spirit who will flood their souls with love for God and their marriage. He causes couples to look away from their own personal issues and give the loving actions that are needed for health and wholeness. Loving actions have the power to heal the individual hurt and pain and restore marital harmony.

When the Spirit-led marriage and family operate by the elements discussed in this chapter, they open themselves to the divine providence of God's miraculous healing and deliverance. He provides a special rush of adrenaline to let their brains act in loving behaviors to their spouses, which, in turn, restores the loving feelings. In addition, if the stresses and marital struggles become unbearable, the Lord will lead couples to Spirit-filled counselors and therapists to help them. Counselors/therapists will walk with them through the process and time for their healing, health, and wholeness. God creates these gifted individuals to provide earthly models to help bring healing and health to marriages and families, and they work in tandem with the Holy Spirit.

Marriage is a gift for couples only in this life. It is a rehearsal and should serve as a model for the heavenly marriage of the Church and the Lamb.

Complete marital and family health comes only from the Author of marriage and family. Therefore, Spirit-led counselors and therapists must also incorporate prayer therapy and Spirit-infilling elements in their practices if true wholeness is to be attained. They must collaboratively enter the therapeutic relationship with a theocentric approach where the Holy Spirit will give instruction and guidance both to the counselor/therapist and the counselees.

Marriage is a gift for couples only in this life. It is a rehearsal and should serve as a model for the heavenly marriage of the Church and the Lamb.

In heaven, we won't need marriage partners. Our heavenly marriage will be consummated at the Marriage Supper of the Lamb. Until then, let us commit ourselves, our marriages, and our families to God in prayer. Let us yield to the Holy Spirit who will love and serve through us and make us epic lovers that others will want to emulate. Let us become epic lovers that are empowered by the Spirit, committed to prayer, willing to invest our time and resources, and are moved with compassion to act in kindness. The endurance of epic lovers' marriages is not sustained by only the four pillars discussed earlier in the chapter. It weathers the challenges of the relationship because of the foundation it was built upon. Let us look at the foundation stones of the epic marriage.

REVIEW QUESTIONS

1. What are the characteristics of an "epic married couple"?
   (1) _____
   (2) _____
   (3) _____

2. What is the main message of Ephesians 5:18 given to married couples?
   _____
   _____
   _____

3. List the EPIC acrostic.
   E – _____
   P – _____
   I – _____
   C – _____

4. According to a data report about divorce, what are two preventers of divorce?
   (1) _____
   (2) _____

5. Showing unconditional love requires a willingness to invest four things. They are:
   _____
   _____
   _____
   _____

END NOTES

[1] Ed Stetzer, president of Lifeway Research Center, article titled, "Pastors: That Divorce Stat You Quoted Is Probably Wrong." In this article, he sheds a great light on how the survey was done. When he looked more deeply at the result, he found the results of divorce among true Bible-believing saints to be much lower.

[2] Gary Thomas, *Sacred Marriage*, (Grand Rapids: Zondervan, 2015).

[3] Frank D. Fincham, "Shifting Toward Cooperative Tendencies and Forgiveness: How Partner-Focused Prayer Transforms Motivation."

[4] Ibid.

[5] Lambert and Fincham, coauthors with C. Nathan DeWall, Richard Pond, and Steven R. Beach, "Shifting Toward Cooperative Tendencies and Forgiveness: How Partner-Focused Prayer Transforms Motivation."

[6] Douglas Small Jr. is the International Prayer coordinator of the Church of God and one of the foremost scholars on prayer.

[7] Benjamin Vima records this in *Prayerfully Yours: Quality Prayer for Quality Life*, p. 43.

[8] "Dr. Tom Ellis, chairman of the Southern Baptist Convention's Council on the Family said that for truly "born-again Christian couples who marry...in the church after having received premarital counseling...and attend church regularly and pray daily together..." experience only one divorce out of nearly 39,000 marriages—or 0.00256 percent. He doubts the accuracy of the Barna poll, noting that "Just saying you are Christian is not going to guarantee that your marriage is going to stay together." One must make a full commitment to God." (http://www.religioustolerance.org/ifm_divo.htm)

[9] Small, Ibid.

[10] Small, Ibid.

[11] Douglas Small, *Prayer—The Heartbeat of the Church* (Cleveland, TN: Pathway Press, 2008), pp. 53-54.

The EPIC MARRIAGE

CHAPTER 2

EPIC MARRIAGE FOUNDATION

Therefore, everyone who hears these words of mine and puts them into practice is like a wise man who built his house on the rock. The rain came down, the streams rose, and the winds blew and beat against that house; yet it did not fall, because it had its foundation on the rock. But everyone who hears these words of mine and does not put them into practice is like a foolish man who built his house on sand. The rain came down, the streams rose, and the winds blew and beat against that house, and it fell with a great crash (Matthew 7:24-27 NIV).

When Mary was a teenager, she surrendered her life to Christ. Despite some bumps and bruises along the way, her walk with the Lord for the past ten years has been a rich and rewarding experience. She has been very involved in her church and has been a blessing to its community.

Secretly however, this beautiful, educated, progressive woman has struggled with emotional challenges since childhood. Although this has been emotionally draining for her, she has developed coping mechanisms to mask her pain and has created a public persona that has gained her the admiration of everyone within her sphere of influence.

Now, at twenty-nine years old, she has met and married a man she considers to be the love of her life, after just two months of friendship.

Mark is a thirty-one-year-old engineer who has just started attending her church. In her words, he is "adorable." She is overjoyed because she believes her "knight in shining armor" has finally come to faith in Christ. Mark has had a checkered past with many questionable episodes. Presently, he is the father of two adorable children with two different women from past relationships. The younger is only a year old. He adores his children and confesses to having only a platonic relationship with both mothers.

The couple received no premarital preparation at all. Mary's family was distraught when they learned about their nuptials. Meanwhile, the church responded with shock at the news of their impending wedding and the leaders tried unsuccessfully to convince them to wait for a while. Many of Mary's peers were heartbroken, not that she was marrying Mark, but with the speed and urgency with which she was being married.

It is now five months since the rushed wedding, and the relationship is under unimaginable stress. It would appear that the ghosts of their pasts have cast a long and haunting shadow over their marriage. The blame game has begun with both individuals engaging in verbal abuse and accusations of deception.

With the existence of this toxic atmosphere, church attendance has been on the decline, and the many stories being circulated in the community are all negative.

Instead of asking for help, they are choosing to stay away from family, friends, and the church.

Importance of a Solid Foundation in Marriage

It has been more than thirty years since my wife, Jenny, and I have been involved in premarital and marriage counseling. Having revealed this truth does not make us marriage experts, but rather students forever learning in the marriage discipleship lab. From here, the story shared at the beginning of this chapter can be multiplied several times. Characters may change, but basic elements are consistent. Why are these kinds of stories so common?

These stories are common because many couples entering marriage are unaware of the need to secure a solid godly foundation, which includes: Blessings from God, the church leaders, the community of faith, parents, and family, as well as support from friends.

When these ingredients are missing at the very foundation of marriage, it creates unnecessary and sometimes unbearable hardships for the couple and their new family. This misguided approach has destroyed many lives. It not only pits spouses against each other, but also innocent children are caught in the middle and are sometimes forced to take sides. More often than not, children are wounded by these experiences as they stand by helplessly while their parents fight and struggle alone without community guidance, support, or help.

Many of these misguided relationships will either terminate their painful relationships, only to contract new ones, thinking new is better, while the children are scarred for life.

Jenny and I have heard many couples say, 'If only I had known then what I know now, I would have done things differently and avoided a lot of heartaches and pains associated with my dysfunctional marriage."

We hope that if your marriage is currently going through undue marital stress because of a faulty beginning, this book will be resourceful in helping you seal and heal some of the foundational cracks in your marriage. God's grace is sufficient to meet all the needs that are brought to Him.

Marriage for a child of God is a divine institution. It is perfect in design and naturally wholesome. However, the popular saying, "Marriages are made in heaven, but they are lived out on earth," is rather appropriate. The reality is that this divine creation is experienced in the context of a broken world. The Creator established this wonderful institution totally conscious of the possible growth experiences or challenges ahead. He made provisions for its sanctity, stability, and sustainability when the right marital building blocks are utilized.

Unfortunately, many Christian couples enter marriage utterly ignorant of this reality. They enter marriage, committing themselves to a lifetime of togetherness, without due diligence. They attempt to establish a healthy marriage lacking a solid godly foundation. Sadly, this is foisted on the premise of unrealistic expectations, ill preparedness, and burdensome baggage. They bring wounded self-images, psychological and emotional scars or trauma, and a faulty understanding of love and genuine commitment dynamics. They try to build a permanent structure on relational shifting sand.

> *Marriage for a child of God is a divine institution. It is perfect in design and naturally wholesome.*

The consequences have been devastating for many couples attempting to build a meaningful relationship in marriage without a proper understanding of how to achieve what God intends for the institution. These couples often start their marriage with a wonderful wedding celebration, euphoric feelings, including a vow to live together with a "happily ever after" expectation. They are usually full

EPIC Marriage Foundation

of hopes and dreams for their future life together. However, they soon discover that this is a major undertaking and that the key to a successful marriage does not come easily and will require resources beyond the human capability.

Today's alarming divorce statistics demonstrate clearly that many couples are finding it difficult to establish the happy marriage they originally set out to build. They are now reaping the bitter harvest of a fast-track relationship which ignored the critical ingredients deemed necessary for establishing a solid foundation, sourced in the Word of God.

We would like to pause and encourage you before you read any further. If you are struggling in your marriage because of a faulty foundation—remember, where you are now, is not the end! God is a God of second chances, even marital ones! The Book of Hosea records Hosea and Gomer's marital struggles that led to separation, and how God gave them a second chance, which was better than their first union (Hosea 1–3).

The first key to having an epic marriage begins with having the right relational foundation. Join us as we journey together and review some building principles that are foundational to the construction of a strong, vibrant, godly, and lasting marriage.

The establishment of an appropriate infrastructure that accommodates a massive structure is one of the most critical underpinnings of building engineering. A strong and solid foundation is a necessity as a preparatory measure, as well as a provision for perpetuity. It serves at least two fundamental purposes as it relates to the building and the ground below.

In the first place, it secures the building in the soil. Second, it serves the critical purpose of protecting the upper walls by transferring the weight of the structure to the soil. These two critical factors account for the stability and durability of some of the world's most astonishing superstructures.

These magnificent buildings rise to remarkable heights and occupy acres of land. Countless millions of tons of concrete and steel have been utilized to create structures that have withstood years of pounding by the elements, natural disasters, traffic, people, etc., because of their firm base. For this to be possible, they have had to be anchored on a firm foundation deep in the ground.

A perfect example of this principle is the Burj Khalifa (Dubai Tower) located in downtown Dubai, United Arab Emirates. Sightseeing in Dubai would be incomplete if one did not visit the tallest manufactured structure in the world.

This magnificent 163-story skyscraper stands 2,722 feet high! Impressive indeed; however, what is seen is not the full extent of the structure. The extensive reinforcement of this structure confounds the layperson and may be seen by many as a waste of resources. The reality is that this structure would not be safe without its extensive foundation. The same can be said of great marriages. The output (visible) is often enviable, but the input (the foundation) is often unseen and therefore unknown.

> As it is with building engineering, "marriage engineering" is a critical undertaking.

As it is with building engineering, "marriage engineering" is a critical undertaking. The integrity of your marriage is a foundational issue. The strength and sustainability of a healthy and Spirit-filled Christian marriage are unmistakably dependent upon the foundation on which they are established. Did you build your marriage on the correct foundation? Are there any cracks? We will address these questions as we look at the building blocks.

EPIC Marriage Foundation

Faith in the God of the Bible is foundational to a strong and epic marriage. Couples commit themselves to God and the covenant of marriage established by His Word. This is the cornerstone to healthy Spirit-filled marriages. However, the opposite is also true. Couples who ignore or disobey the "marriage building code" by failing to establish a solid footing are at risk as they seek to construct a strong and healthy marriage and family.

How do we adequately illustrate the need for a solid foundation in marriage? The parable of the "Wise and Foolish Builder" (Matthew 7:24-27) appropriately illustrates this point. Our Lord, in His own unique style, cites an example from building engineering to provide a lesson in contrasts. He reinforced the notion that the integrity of the structures depends undeniably upon the foundation. The building, no matter how impressive, stands or falls on the integrity of its foundation.

So then, what accounts for the brokenness and horrifying challenges being experienced in millions of Christian marriages globally? Many have concluded that something is wrong with the biblical marriage model.

Some view it as archaic and out of touch with current postmodern realities. That is one opinion. We do not believe that the problem is marriage in and of itself. Rather, it is couples entering the institution without laying the right foundation for the construction of a long and lasting marriage. The problem is, their approach is defective.

> *Most Christian marriages fail because of inadequate or incorrect anchoring.*

Most Christian marriages fail because of inadequate or incorrect anchoring. This is exemplified as we saw earlier in the story with Mary and Mark. Many of the struggles they were experiencing are emblematic of feeble attempts by couples trying desperately to control the proverbial "cart before the horse." Since Mary and Mark did not have the proper marital foundation, their marital conflicts short-circuited their Romantic Love stage and catapulted into Stage 2—Faultfinding—"You are flawed."

The correct marital foundation will provide the anchor for couples to navigate each marital stage successfully and build more sound marriages. Building on each stage is necessary to sustain a long and lasting marriage (see Chapter 9 of *The Love Factor in Marriage* published by Creation House Publishing). Unless Mary and Mark receive counseling to address the baggage in their marriage, their unhealthy relationship could precipitously degenerate into a state of mediocrity, separation, and eventually divorce. Each marital stage is very important for couples to go through, because they are building blocks that lead to the level of acceptance and harmonious living.

It is sad to see the alarming number of couples who are being sidetracked by the symptoms of marital instability and who end up chasing the wind like Mary and Mark. It is even more alarming that many experts, such as counselors and therapists, are just as puzzled as their clients. Rather than attempting to remedy the "people problem" of marriage, they spend their time trying to redefine marriage.

This is a phantom pursuit. Can you see the implications of the redefinition of marriage? If we continue on this trajectory, we will have to continue redefining marriage again and again to satiate the trends, fads, and *zeitgeist*.[1] However, we must never forget that it is God and God alone who has the inalienable right to modify, redefine, or reconstruct the institution of marriage. Why? He created it.

Contrary to the notion that there is something fundamentally wrong with marriage, as taught by some faith groups and pop culture, there is nothing wrong with marriage. The problem is not with marriage, but with the inability of couples to begin with the correct foundation.

Manufacturers provide operational guidelines for every gadget we purchase today. They warn that these be read prior to the use of the product and be adhered to during operation. These owner's manuals are provided to protect the equipment from the ignorant, as well as the arrogant. We are warned that the product should be used for no other purpose and in no other way than for which it was designed.

Manufacturers are unforgiving in this regard. Warranty is nullified if we disregard the instructions, and then we are forced to take responsibility for our actions. They guarantee that if we operate the product as designed, it will function properly.

An interesting observation is to compare the reviews of various products, whether cars, computers, or mobile phones. It is fascinating that one person expresses reservations about the item in question, while another promotes it with unrestrained commendations, and their sentiments aren't unsupported. They have the antique car to prove the point.

Many marriages have gone the distance. Couples have grown old together. They have been through similar or even worse experiences than many whose marriages ended in divorce. Listening to their stories has often moved many to tears and also been the source of inspiration to many couples seeking to restore wounded relationships.

It is critical that we Spirit-filled believers revisit the owner's manual, the Bible, to rediscover its guidelines for Spirit-filled marriages and recommit to abide by its instructions.

Likewise, focus needs to be placed on equipping the many Marys and Marks of our culture with tools for reestablishing healthy, Spirit-filled relationships, prior to contracting a marriage, as well as providing support for those who are already married without having a proper foundation.

The latter usually requires a delicate undertaking that may necessitate counseling, therapy, and healing from God. However, by God's grace, they too can experience healthy marriages.

An excellent place to begin this journey is to conduct an inventory of the elements of a Spirit-filled marriage foundation.

It is critical that we Spirit-filled believers revisit the owner's manual, the Bible, to rediscover its guidelines for Spirit-filled marriages and recommit to abide by its instructions.

The Elements of a Spirit-filled Marital Foundation

Getting married is one of the most significant, life-changing events one will ever encounter. Unfortunately, many couples are totally oblivious to this reality. Unconsciously, they exert so much effort planning for their glorious wedding day, while totally disregarding or taking for granted those far more crucial years that comprise the lifetime of love we all promise and pursue. At the outset of their marital lives, most couples *take for granted* that their marriage will just work automatically, no matter the impending challenges.

The reality is, marriage is uncharted territory for most couples, and they do not have the knowledge or skill sets to build a successful marriage. Unfortunately, many have not had great relationships modeled before their eyes. Few couples have been adequately prepared for this major undertaking by family, church, or society. Therefore, many couples are ignorant of the importance of a secure anchorage. However, without God at its foundation, they become an accident waiting to happen. Why? The structural durability of their marriage is contingent on God—the foundation.

Many couples approach marriage as an event, but the truth is, marriage is not simply an event, but a process. The wedding day with all its trappings and excitement, is not the main event. It has an end date. Marriage is a permanent process that breaks at death. It is not built instantly, but incrementally. It requires the solid, godly foundation on which a permanent structure can be erected and sustained. The base of healthy Spirit-filled relationships is God himself. The cornerstones of this foundation that God has laid in His Word are: one's love for God, self, and others, and commitment to the covenant of marriage, which is made possible with only the enabling connection of the Holy Spirit.

When individuals fail to establish their love for God, for self, and for others, before marriage, they can compromise the structural integrity of the relationship, thereby threatening its stability and sustainability. The elements of a solid marital foundation need to be examined next.

> *Many couples approach marriage as an event, but the truth is, marriage is not simply an event, but a process.*

Love for God

The love command (*schema*)[2] in Deuteronomy 6:5— "Love the LORD your God with all your heart and with all your soul and with all your strength" (NIV)—clearly indicates the profound appreciation and adoration that God requires from all peoples, but dare we say, more so from couples. It also indicates that, as it relates to our affection and emotions, God is to be given priority. This is critical, because on this hinges all other expressions of our love and devotion. The reality is that loving others adequately is evidence of love for God (See Weaver p. 1). Love for God is demonstrated by love for the other.[4]

While it is true that many marriage conflicts are resolved out of expediency, economic reasons, children, and social pressures, it is also true that love for God is a powerful stabilizing factor in countless relationships.

Knowing what God requires and desiring to fulfill His will at all times becomes the deal breaker for many couples experiencing marriage deadlock. Had some couples observed this critical element prior to marriage, their relationship would not have ended up on the rocks.

First John 4:20-21 provides our support for this position. John says,

> If anyone says, "I love God," yet hates his brother, he is a liar; for he who does not love his brother, whom he has seen, cannot love God, whom he has not seen. And this commandment we have from him: Whoever loves God must also love his brother (ESV).

The above verse tells couples they must devote themselves to unrestrained love for God, which removes hatred of brothers. This should involve their entire being, intellect, emotion, and spirit. It was stated that love for God is demonstrated by love for our partners. However, as mentioned above, this love finds expression in loving the other correctly, and love for the other is to be congruent to love for self. This is achieved as we commit ourselves to Him in submission and obedience.

One's love and commitment to God is therefore reflected in the relationship. It is a critical foundational element—excluding uncompromised commitment to loving God first in the relationship is a recipe for disaster. The biblical marriage model outlined in Genesis 1 and 2, revealed that Adam had the opportunity to develop a love relationship with God first, before he was given a wife. This leads us to our second foundational element—love for others.

Love for Others

The notion of love for the other is fundamental to Scripture. The Bible cites at least three compelling reasons for loving one another. First, we are all created in the image of God. Second, this reality establishes our equality before God. Third, the Bible teaches the universal fatherhood of God which presupposes the universal brotherhood of man (Acts 17:26—"From one man he made every nation of the human race to inhabit the entire earth" NET). These three compelling realities urge our appreciation for the other in a most significant way and provide the Spirit-filled Christian couple with amazing security.

However, one may ask: How do we appropriately demonstrate love for others without denying ourselves in some significant way? The following biblical injunctions eloquently answer this question:

1. Love your neighbor as yourself (Leviticus 19:18; Matthew 19:19; 22:37-39; Romans 13:8-10; Galatians 5:14-15).
2. Husbands ought to love their wives as their own bodies (Ephesians 5:28).
3. Do to others what you would have them do to you (Matthew 7:12).

These love commands indicate that without a proper appreciation of the self, one cannot properly value the other. It is interesting to note that the injunctions seem to present "self-love" as the paradigm for "other love," neighbor, or partner. The neighbor is to be loved "as self." The wives are to be loved as the husband's "own body." In other words, the care that a husband has for his personal comfort should be consistent with that which he displays toward his wife.

It is further noted that not only should the neighbor be loved as one's own self and the wife be loved as the husband's own body, but also our actions toward others should be motivated by that which we would desire them to do to us. We should treat our partners the same as we expect to be treated by them.

The key lies in our understanding that loving the self appropriately offers the prototype for proper love for others. This is huge for a Spirit-filled Christian couple. Understanding this and appropriating it in a marriage can make all the difference. It would be the antidote for the plethora of ills plaguing many marriages today: cheating, lying, abuse, deception, selfishness, and the list goes on.

The critical question that may be asked is: How is this accomplished in an age characterized by rapid change, narcissism, selfishness, and individualism? It is only possible when couples allow the Holy Spirit to lead their lives.

Love of Self

From the foregoing, it is critical for individuals to personally understand the order of love if they are going to be able to appropriate the right kind of love to their neighbors. This understanding of loving self in relation to neighbor and loving neighbor in relation to self is the key to a better appreciation of self and others. Loving self authentically in our postmodern culture that is characterized by individualism, narcissism, greed, and selfishness, does require consideration, but we cannot do justice to the subject here.

To help us appreciate the love command, we need to look at two of the love commands in Scripture which seem to suggest that self-love is a model of love for others.

The oft reiterated, "love your neighbor as yourself" motif, does not stand alone in this category. Men are instructed in Ephesians 5:28 to love their wives as their own bodies.

If we do not understand self-love, we will be our own archenemy. We will inadvertently relate to our partner and others based on our perception of reality. Consequently, others will know the value we have placed on ourselves and treat us accordingly. Therefore, it must be repeated that loving self appropriately provides the model for proper love for others—one's partner being the most significant. A healthy love of self must first be attained before one can truly love others. It can only be achieved when we make God's love our number one.

This love model was a command given in Deuteronomy to the Jews and later repeated in the New Testament church. However, we need to emphasize that this was not new in biblical practice.

In the Genesis account of Creation, we see this model exemplified in the first human couple. When God made Adam and Eve, in Genesis 1:25-28; 2:21-25, He created them with a perfect love for God, self, and others.

Genesis 3:8 tells us that God came walking in the Garden

> *If we do not understand self-love, we will be our own archenemy. We will inadvertently relate to our partner and others based on our perception of reality.*

and communicated with Adam in the cool of the day. It is clear from this statement that Adam had an excellent relationship with God, evidenced by the fact that He could identify his voice. He had a wonderful love relationship with God.

Adam also had a perfect love for himself. He was satisfied with the person he was created to be. He was comfortable in himself and embraced his role as the gardener of Eden. Adam appreciated his purpose and function in life as the custodian of Paradise and all that God had put him in charge of. However, Adam not only had a healthy appreciation of self-love, but also he was created with the capacity to look beyond himself and extend his love to others. This was clearly seen in his acceptance of Eve when God presented her to him as his wife, he quickly acknowledged her as his equal companion and helpmate. He took her as his wife, and the two became one flesh.

Sin is the culprit that marred the perfect love relationship between God, self, and others. The second Adam, Jesus Christ, through His vicarious death and resurrection effectively paved the way for the restoration of that love relationship. Today, believers who have accepted Jesus Christ as Savior and Lord and have allowed the Holy Spirit to continually fill their lives daily will live in a wonderful relationship of love with God, love of self, and love of others.

Commitment to the Marriage Covenant

Finally, another critical element of the Spirit-filled Christian marriage is the commitment to our spouses and marriage covenant. Without this building block, the security and endurance of the relationship is unsustainable. Persons who are ignorant of this reality often do not place a high premium on their relationship. Consequently, inappropriate, compromising, and attitudinal behaviors that would normally and unceremoniously be repudiated become the norm.

The Scriptures are clear regarding God's abhorrence for the breaking of the sacred marriage covenant. Yahweh constantly rebuked His people for disobeying the covenant relationship He had established with them by employing the clear and compelling imagery of the marriage covenant. From these, we can find valuable principles that reveal God's position and passion for the marriage covenant.

The prophet Malachi, for example, provided guidance in this regard for the people of Israel. He expressed God's utter disgust for the breaking of the marriage covenant. In rather moving terms, he declares God's hatred toward this behavior. He advises the male partner that God was displeased because he had "broken faith" with "the wife of [his] youth." He admonished on two occasions to "guard yourself in your spirit, and do not break faith with the wife of your youth" (see Malachi 2:14-15).

Yahweh constantly rebuked His people for disobeying the covenant relationship He had established with them by employing the clear and compelling imagery of the marriage covenant.

Malachi's exhortation introduces a critical point to our discussion: "…guard yourself in your spirit" (v. 15). This reminds us of the spiritual dimension of the marriage. This is critical for this discourse since it is our firm conviction that marriage is a creation of the Spirit of God and is sustained by the Holy Spirit. As such, partners need the guidance of the Holy Spirit in order not to "break faith."

> Another thing you do: You flood the Lord's altar with tears. You weep and wail because he no longer pays attention to your offerings or accepts

them with pleasure from your hands. You ask, "Why?" It is because the LORD is acting as the witness between you and the wife of your youth, because **you have broken faith** with her, though she is your partner, **the wife of your marriage covenant.** Has not [the LORD] made them one? In flesh and spirit, they are his. And why one? He was seeking godly offspring. So, guard yourself in your spirit, and do not break faith with the wife of your youth." "I hate divorce," says the LORD God of Israel, "and I hate a man's covering himself with violence as well as with his garment," says the LORD Almighty. So, guard yourself in your spirit, and do not break faith (Malachi 2:13-16 NIV).

Jesus also addresses the sanctity of the marriage covenant. He, more than anyone else, stressed the permanence of the covenant and the spiritual bond that exists in the heterosexual marriage. In Matthew 19:4-6, Jesus urged:

> "Haven't you read," he replied, "that at the beginning the Creator 'made them male and female,' and said, 'For this reason a man will leave his father and mother and be united to his wife, and the two will become one flesh'? So, they are no longer two, but one. Therefore, what God has joined together, let man not separate" (NIV).

Again, in Matthew 22:37-39,

> Jesus replied: "'Love the Lord your God with all your heart and with all your soul and with all your mind.' This is the first and greatest commandment. And the second is like it: 'Love your neighbor as yourself' (NIV).

God, love, and commitment to the covenant of marriage are stepping stones to Spirit-filled marriages. How Christians view God, practice love, and the level of commitment they have toward marriage reveal the kind of marriage relationship they will have.

We should note that God designed marriage to function for the health and welfare of husbands, wives, and families. We will now look at the different kinds of marriages.

There are four kinds of marriages:
1. The Perfect Marriage
2. The False Marriage
3. The Fairytale Marriage
4. The Real Marriage

The Perfect Marriage

Many couples would like to live in a perfect marriage; however, that is not possible in this lifetime. There is only one way couples can live and flourish in a perfect marriage—they need to have a perfect environment first. God created a perfect environment—Eden—for the first couple. In Eden, there was no sin. Adam and Eve were the only couple that ever lived in a perfect marriage.

Adam and Eve were created at different times to fulfill a divine design. I wish I could tell you with certainty what that design was; however, I cannot. According to the Genesis account of Creation, God created every animal in pairs. However, He did not create Adam and Eve as a pair. Instead, He created Adam, and when He was finished, God said, "It is not good for the man to be alone. I will make a helper suitable for him" (Genesis 2:18 NIV). What was missing in Adam's life was a suitable companion with whom he could share a lifetime of love, commitment, intimacy, and passion.

Without Eve, Adam had no one with whom he could share himself physically. Eve fulfilled the missing portion of the equation of God's design for Adam to experience passion, intimacy, pleasure, and procreation. God designed man and woman to live in pure and perfect intimacy, passion, and commitment when He said, "For this reason a man will leave his father and mother and be united to his wife, and they will become one flesh. The man and his wife were both naked, and they felt no shame" (Genesis 2:24–25 NIV). Eve became Adam's sexual partner, for the text declares Adam united to his wife, Eve, in total and perfect intimacy, free from fear, guilt, and shame.

> *A lifestyle of faulty intimacy guarantees a false marriage. It is a self-created illusion to help couples avoid the pains inherent in real marital intimacy.*

All couples are now living in a sinful environment, and we must learn how to live in this sinful world, glorify God, and create and maintain the epic marriage God wants. If there is no perfect marriage, what kind of marriages do we have?

The False Marriage

Is my marriage a false one? A lifestyle of faulty intimacy guarantees a false marriage. It is a self-created illusion to help couples avoid the pains inherent in real marital intimacy. Many couples choose false intimacy because they do not want to experience pain and hurt that comes with being vulnerable. Pain, hurt, guilt, and shame in marriage are inherent in all marriages because of sin.

For couples who are tired of living in a marriage with the false sense of intimacy, there is hope. Open yourself to the infilling of the Holy Spirit, and He will give you the power to expose your true self to each other; and then through the vulnerable moments, you both will grow and build a better intimacy. You may have been married for many years; but, if you are living in a false marriage with false intimacy, you do not need to remain there.

The Fairytale Marriage

The Prince of Wales, Charles, and Diana's marriage was one of the most watched weddings in the 20th century. Many people who watched the wedding expected that one day, Prince Charles and Diana would ascend the throne to replace Queen Elizabeth II. But that was only a fairytale expectation.

Fairytale marriages are where a princess and her Prince Charming get married and ride off into couplehood, expecting to live "happily ever after."

The message conveyed in a fairytale marriage is, love leads to wedding, and married life leads to lasting happiness. Fairytale marriages exist only in one's imagination. They are not real. Fairytale marriage expectations insinuate that all problems will disappear once Mr. or Mrs. Right comes along. That is only a dream.

> *There is no perfect spouse. Each person entering marriage needs to understand that fact clearly; because, each partner enters the relationship with different levels of imperfections, limitations, and flaws.*

Another issue with the fairytale marriage is, couples usually believe they find and marry their perfect partner. There is no perfect spouse. Each person entering marriage needs to understand that fact clearly; because, each partner enters the relationship with different levels of imperfections, limitations, and flaws. But with love, commitment, knowledge, patience, time, support, and God, they will help each other to lead a meaningful and productive life, which makes for a fulfilling and rewarding epic marriage. Fairytale marriages are for young, dreaming children. Finally, we will examine the last kind of marriage.

The Real Marriage

Often, we who are involved in marriage and family ministry would hear some of our clients in our practices say, "Couple romance dies, and relationships tend to go sour after two years." This is true in some marriages; however, it does not have to be true in a Spirit-filled marriage.

"Why?" you ask! We need to consider this question with another one.

"Can you remember how your relationship started?" Regardless if your answer is yes or no, it is believed in the Western culture that marriage relationships usually begin with loving connections or chemistry attractions.

In most cases, this loving connection or chemistry attraction was watered by loving behaviors and actions. One possible reason some relationships go sour may be caused by a problem with chemistry. Chemistry may ebb and flow by moods, hormones, medications, and feelings. But when couples intentionally choose to constantly water their relationship with loving actions and behaviors, it creates a more pleasurable roller coaster ride. This is the real marriage. In a real marriage, Spirit-filled couples intentionally work to build their relationship through the things they say and do for each other continually.

> *In a real marriage, Spirit-filled couples intentionally work to build their relationship through the things they say and do for each other continually.*

In a real marriage, Spirit-filled couples commit themselves and their marriages to God through daily personal and couple prayer, as well as Bible-reading practices. They build and use their altar in the home to commune with God. Their daily prayer and Bible reading open them up to the infusion of the Holy Spirit. Through these daily times with God, couples are empowered to love and serve each other and display the glory of God in their everyday activities in the good and not so good experiences!

When we speak of real marriage, "what do we mean?" We would like to use an acrostic to list four main elements that must be in a real marriage. In a real marriage that is guided by the Holy Spirit, couples commit themselves to intentionally show *respect* to each other, be *empathetic* to each other, *adapt* to their growth, and fully commit to grow in *love*.

R – Respect
E – Empathetic
A – Adapt
L – Love

Respect

Soul singer and music icon Aretha Franklin is a preacher's daughter. She began her singing career in the church, but at age eighteen, she switched from gospel to secular music. In 1967, she recorded a song titled "RESPECT." This song while highlighting the cry of a woman to her lover for respect was also an anthem or a rallying cry for those during the Civil Rights Movement to have the political directorate of their day treat them with respect. What is respect? The word *respect* means "to esteem, honor, and value another." Too many relationships disintegrate, because there is a lack of respect between spouses. No relationship can exist, nurture, grow, and develop without respect. Respect is the cornerstone of any fledging, meaningful relationship and even more so a real marriage! It is the breath that gives life to the marriage. It plays a central role in the foundation of the marriage troth. It began before the wedding day and continues and grows through the stages of married life.

- People can become violent if they think that someone "dissed" them or treated them with a lack of respect.
- Without respect in marriage, the marriage will go sour and result in the eventual disillusionment of the marriage.

Why does respect play such a pivotal role? It plays a pivotal role because in a real marriage, each partner in the relationship lives to honor and respect the gift—the husband or wife God has created and given to them for life. When couples express honor and esteem to each other, they are dignifying the Creator's design. They are honoring and displaying the character, the image, and the likeness of God.

What does it mean to have respect in marriage? It means: "to view or consider each other with a degree of reverence; to esteem each other as possessor of real worth." "It is the estimation or honor in which couples hold the distinguished worth or substantial good qualities of others. Respect regards the qualities of the mind, or the actions which characterize their partners."[3]

Many people combine love and respect together. For this book, I will address both under their own heading. Many people believe they go together like a horse and carriage and without both, marriage will crumble. Like, Dr. Emerson Eggerich's book, *Love and Respect,* he said: "They go together." He explains

When couples express honor and esteem to each other, they are dignifying the Creator's design.

it by saying, "When a husband shows love for his wife that motivates her respect. When a wife shows respect for her husband that motivates his love." As shown in the following illustration:[4]

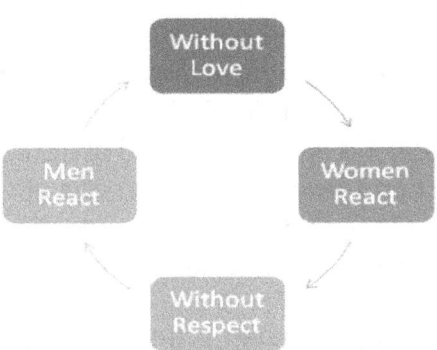

True, they work together! But, they are two of the four building blocks of real marriage.

Both are to be practiced in marriage, but they are two distinct entities.

In real marriage, respect is practiced by both partners. It is mutually given and received. It means that couples treat each other in a thoughtful and courteous way. Mutual respect means that couples view their opinions, wishes, and values as worthy of serious consideration.

The Bible calls us to mutual respect, when the apostle Paul writes, "Fulfil ye my joy, that ye be likeminded, having the same love, being of one accord, of one mind. Let nothing be done through strife or vainglory; but in lowliness of mind let each esteem other better than themselves" (Philippians 2:2-3 KJV).

Jesus teaches all believers, but more so, loving couples, when He said, "And as ye would that men should do to you, do ye also to them likewise" (Luke 6:31 KJV). That is respect

... Jesus was calling for mutual respect between couples and this was an unconditional requirement.

Each spouse is seen and given full right to function in the union as God created him/her to, not as stereotype, but each one can use his/her gifts and talents to advance the marriage. Spirit-filled couples respect the differences that God has placed in each spouse. They choose to use the differences to help bring balance to their relationship, rather than seeking compliance and uniformity. They take time to honor and revere each other as a gift of God. They admire each other and value their opinion. They are respected as individuals with their own personalities and as a corporate whole.

While infusing our relationships with respect may be challenging, and at times hard to define, it is critical for any healthy relationship. Generally, respect is present when we embrace the concepts of acceptance and forgiveness, allowing another to make mistakes without judging their motives, while listening and appreciating their unique personalities. We treat others honorably, listening to them and valuing their points of view. We are sensitive to the boundaries they have established.

Empathy

Empathy is another key ingredient that couples in real marriage use to understand each other and grow in love. Christian couples searching to find biblical support for the word *empathy* in the Bible will be disappointed, because it is not mentioned; however, take comfort, the characteristic of demonstrating empathy runs all through the pages of Scripture.

The Bible talks much about, "sharing another's emotions and feelings," when it says, "Have compassion for one another; love as brothers, be tenderhearted, be courteous"

(1 Peter 3:8 NKJV). "Rejoice with those who rejoice, and weep with those who weep" (Romans 12:15 NKJV).

Then, there are five references to Jesus being moved with compassion: Matthew 9:36; 14:14; 18:27; Mark 1:41; 6:34. These scriptures are key guides to motivate Spirit-filled couples to live in the real marriage and walk in each other's shoes.

Success in real marriages does not rest upon what a spouse can get, but more so, upon what a spouse is willing to share—intimately share! The gift of empathy in a real marriage creates a sense of oneness in marriage unlike many other gifts couples can give to their spouses.

Empathy is the capacity in marriage to feel deeply for your spouse, so you can identify with his/her feelings and needs. It is the key that unlocks the door to our kindness and compassion for our mates. The gift of empathy helps create good listeners in marriage. Couples take time to fully attend to the needs of each other, even if it requires putting one's own needs aside. Empathy is being able to relate with and understand the feelings of your partner. It is putting yourself in your spouse's shoes so you can identify with their experience.

Empathy develops a spirit of connectivity and bond in the real marriage. Empathy connects us so there is a feeling of oneness. This connection gives couples the permission to empathize by crying together and sharing their sorrows and joys together. When couples can share, and understand their mate's feelings, needs, concerns, and emotional state, they are able to communicate on a level which will facilitate loving actions, as well as comfort.

> *Success in real marriages does not rest upon what a spouse can get, but more so, upon what a spouse is willing to share—intimately share!*

Why is empathy so important in marriage? If every couple chooses to empathize with each other, marriages in our society would be much healthier and divorce would be significantly less. Lianne Choo wrote an article titled, "7 Reasons Why Empathy Is Important in a Relationship." She said empathy helps:

(1) Bridge the divide.
(2) Give each other attention.
(3) Bring out the positive.
(4) Practice compassion.
(5) Walk a mile in someone else's shoes.
(6) Teach patience.
(7) Work on your flaws.

She closed the article by saying, "Self-awareness and a non-judgmental attitude is needed before you can properly empathize with someone." She further said, "Look within yourself and find the strength to be less selfish and more understanding, and you are well on your way to connecting better with your loved ones."[5]

In a real marriage, empathy makes couples become more reflective listeners and they seek to practice the three A's of empathy, which are (1) awareness, (2) agenda, and (3) action.[6]

If you recognize the need to better empathize with your spouse, consider these three A's to feel empathy:

- **Awareness**—Be aware of what your spouse is feeling and what is behind that feeling.
- **Agenda**—Set aside your own agenda and focus on the needs of your spouse.
- **Action**—Take action on meeting the needs of your spouse.

Most of Jesus' miracles were motivated by empathy or a more biblical word— compassion. Using empathy is practice in marriage, in healing, and in salvific ways.

Adaptability

In real marriage, couples are constantly learning to adapt to the nonessentials and remain firm to the essentials. Married couples are cognizant of the fact that as time progresses, they need to make and adapt to changes that will facilitate growth in their marriages. The house chores will change. Husbands and children may be required to do some or more household chores than they ever intended. This is just another part of the marital dynamics. As couples and families, we need to be pliable and flexible as we deal with the changes in our relationships. We adapt to changes and things all the time even when we are unaware. So, when life changes, apply those same skills in your marriages that you use in your everyday living.

Healthy marriages and families must develop predictable routines, roles, and rules that govern everyday life and provide for continuity and stability. However, the varied circumstances around marriage and family life may necessitate individual adaptation. Since no family knows what tomorrow will bring, being adaptive and flexible is a good trait for family members to develop.

> *In real marriage, couples are constantly learning to adapt to the nonessentials and remain firm to the essentials.*

In the book, *Family: A Christian Perspective on the Contemporary Home,* Jack and Judith Balswick addressed four major characteristics of marriage (Balswick and Balswick 2014). The four characteristics are: commitment, adaptability, authority, and communication.[7]

Most of the time families with a good balance of structure and flexibility (neither overly rigid nor chaotic) are the most effective.[8]

They mentioned, when a man and a woman come together in marriage, they bring with them at times role expectations or predetermined gender roles. These role expectations are not always predetermined by an agreement between spouses. It is suggested by Jack and Judith Balswick that "roles be clearly defined but interchangeable in terms of gender and subject to change."[9] They further stated, that "determining roles through agreement opens up creative possibilities for husbands and wives to serve each other through their roles."[10]

Epic marriages turn these changes into growth for the betterment of relationship. Balswick added, "Life has certain changes that are inevitable, especially in marriage and family life and couples need to be flexible, adapt, and have interchangeable roles when the occasion calls for it."[11]

Real marriage is adaptable; it grows and molds itself to the environment and current needs. It changes as the partners grow, shifting over time and over the stages of marriage and life transitions. Couples living in a real marriage acquire a growth mindset. Both partners are motivated to grow, learn, and develop, both corporately and individually, as well as believe that they will improve themselves and the union for better. Growth ensures that a marriage remains robust, relevant, and useful.

It accepts that people change over time and with experience. In an adaptable marriage, each partner remains curious about the other and limits assumptions and premature conclusions.

Love

Couples living in real marriage, with real love, do not build their love off euphoric, spontaneous feeling—instead they consider love as a deliberate choice—a plan to love each other for better or worse, for richer or poorer, in sickness and in health. Western couples in many cases do not choose who they are attracted to, but they choose who they will love and *stay* in love with. Some people believe, "No one falls in love by choice, it is by chance. No one stays in love by chance; it is accomplished by work. And no one falls out of love by chance; it is by choice."

Real love for the epic marriage asks us to do hard things—to forgive one another, to support each other's dreams, to comfort in times of grief, or to care for family. Real love is not easy—and it is nothing like the wedding day—but it is far more meaningful and wonderful. The apostle Paul explains real love in 1 Corinthians 13:4-13. While researching about Paul's view on love, I, Daniel, came upon an article, on *Bible.org*, Lesson 12: "Working in Love and Loving at Work" (1 Thessalonians 4:9-12). In this article, the following list appeared, but I have modified it to apply to marriage relationship. To each description, we should ask ourselves the question attached and evaluate the answer. We hope this will help us to grow in love.

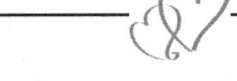

Real marriage is adaptable; it grows and molds itself to the environment and current needs.

- *"Love is patient."* Would my spouse or family describe me as a patient lover? Do I have a "short fuse"?
- *"Love is kind."* Am I kind and gracious toward my spouse, family, and others, especially if he or she falls short of my expectations?

- *"Love is not jealous."* Am I encouraging my spouse to grow and be better?
- *"Love does not brag and is not arrogant."* Am I self-focused, always trying to impress my spouse with my achievements, my opinions, or my knowledge?
- *"Love does not act unbecomingly."* Am I rude to my spouse? Do I often interrupt my spouse? Am I considerate of his/her feelings and points-of-view?
- *"Love does not seek its own."* Am I selfish? Do I think about the needs of my spouse ahead of my own?
- *"Love is not provoked."* Am I easily offended when my spouse expresses his/her disappointments? Do I get angry when my spouse doesn't do what I want him/her to do?
- *"Love does not take into account a wrong suffered."* Do I keep score? Do I remind my partner of his/her past sins or failures? Do I hold grudges? Am I quick to forgive?
- *"Love does not rejoice in unrighteousness but rejoices in the truth."* Am I glad when my spouse fails or sins, because it makes me look good and I can use it as ammunition against him/her? Am I truly happy when I hear of my spouse's victories in the Lord?
- *"Love bears all things."* Do I bear with my spouse in his/her immaturity or shortcomings, or do I always correct him/her?
- *"Love believes all things."* Am I suspicious of my spouse? Do I trust him/her unless there is good reason not to do so?
- *"Love hopes all things."* Do I "write my spouse off because of constant mistakes"? Do I believe that God can work to change my spouse when he/she fails?

- *"Love never fails."* Do I give up on my spouse when he/she has wronged or hurt me? Am I committed to helping my spouse become all that God wants him or her to be?[12]

Your answers to these questions were not meant to measure how much you love. Instead, they are supposed to help you grow in real love daily. On the other hand, it does not matter what others might think of the answers to the questions, it matters more to you and God. Remember, there's always room to grow because our standard is none other than the Lord Jesus Christ.

To achieve a fulfilling, meaningful, and truly happy marriage, couples need to choose to love at all times. Do not just wait for the right times or feelings to show love. Create the times, and feelings will follow. One way to achieve this is to develop a habit of lovingly doing things for each other.

You may be asking, why it is that this is the shortest section? It is because, if the choice is made to love and pursue, all the literary exposé will not be necessary.

Now that you have read about the different types of marriages, I trust that you will endeavor to choose the REAL marriage. The real marriage is not perfect. It is a work in progress. It is a marriage that requires action and the presence and empowerment of the Holy Spirit.

The traditional marriage, as we know it, is a challenging experience for many couples. In fact, marriage, whether by choice or arranged, is under attack. The devil is determined to destroy marriages, which are the backbone of society. We cannot allow him to eliminate God's gift to humanity. God designed marriage as a union where each partner could experience growth and become a healing agent through love.

In order for couples to build a healthy loving marriage, they must intentionally determine the kind of mate they will be, and the kind of marital relationship they will create and work hard at it daily.

Some couples would blame our high rate of marital failure on things like:

- Not spending enough quality time together
- Allowing bitterness and resentment to build in their hearts
- Failing to keep communication lines open
- Unrealistic and unreasonable expectations
- Proposals of male/female differences

There are credible data to support these claims, but in a real Spirit-filled marriage, where the Holy Spirit is Lord, He will supply the wisdom and love that will be needed daily to address all the marital issues and use them to build stronger marriages and reveal the glory of God in your marriage.

> ...an epic marriage becomes a school of discipleship, where couples live and work daily to produce Christ-centered character...

Having now examined the foundation of a healthy marriage relationship, let us now turn our attention to the following chapters that will discuss some primary building materials that is needed in the Spirit-filled marriage and family.

A real epic marriage is not known first and foremost by outward appearances. No, they are not! Many couples wear a public persona of having epic marriages, but a closer look at their children, and their personal lives show the opposite.

When it is all said and done, an epic marriage becomes a school of discipleship, where couples live and work daily to produce Christ-centered character living and loving children who when ready to create their own like-manner EPIC marriage will use the parents as a good model and guide for their own marriage. The following chapters will help provide guidance to having an epic marriage.

In building engineering, items such as steel and concrete are essential for the establishment of a stable and sustainable base for superstructures; likewise, the marriage relationship requires durable underpinning, or it will not withstand the changes of life. God is the foundation of a lasting marriage. Love for Him, others, and self, as well as commitment to Him and the covenant of marriage are indispensable elements of that foundation. When these cornerstones are laid, the Spirit-filled marriage will be the real marriage that couples will commit to work toward daily.

The EPIC MARRIAGE

REVIEW QUESTIONS

1. List three blessings that should be ascertained before the consummation of an epic marriage.
   a. _____
   b. _____
   c. _____

2. In what ways do couples build their marital relationships on shifting ground?
   a. _____
   b. _____
   c. _____

3. Why is faith in the God of the Bible so foundational to a strong and epic marriage?
   _____
   _____
   _____

4. Fill in the blank and explain the statement. Marriage is not simply an _____ but a _____.

5. List the three elements of a Spirit-filled, marital foundation, and discuss why a person needs to master them prior to entering marriage?
   a. _____
   b. _____
   c. _____

6. List and discuss the four kinds of marriages.
   a. _____
   b. _____
   c. _____

EPIC Marriage Foundation

7. In real marriages, couples commit themselves to:
   a. _____
   b. _____
   c. _____

END NOTES

[1] *Zeitgeist* refers to "the spirit or mood of a particular period of history as shown by the ideas and beliefs of the time."

[2] Schema describes a pattern of thought, a mental structure of preconceived ideas, a framework representing some aspect of the world or behavior that organizes categories of information and the relationships among them.

[3] Darlene Fozard Weaver, *Self-Love and Christian Ethic*, (Cambridge University Press, November 2002).

[4] Dr. Emerson Eggerichs, *Love and Respect*, (Nashville: Thomas Nelson, 2009).

[5] http://www.lovepanky.com/love-couch/better-love/reasons-why-empathy-is-important-in-a-relationship.

[6] http://www.markmerrill.com/3-as-of-empathy-for-your-marriage.

[7] Balswick, Jack O. and Judith K. Balswick. *The Family: A Christian Perspective on the Contemporary Home* (Grand Rapids: Baker Academic, 2014).

[8] Ibid

[9] Ibid

[10] Ibid

[11] Ibid.

[12] Adapted from Bible.org, https://bible.org/seriespage/lesson-12-working-love-and-loving-work-1-thessalonians-49-12.

CHAPTER 3

A LOVE PROMISE WORTH KEEPING!

After the honeymoon period ends, the euphoric feelings of new love often fades and the relationship between epic married couples evolves into a deeper and more committed quality of love. The reality is, marriage is not just about the emotional butterflies and euphoria associated with romantic love. Although love is one of the main ingredients for a long-lasting relationship, it eventually changes and takes on different forms.

With the passage of time, love is metamorphosed into deeper levels of intimacy, friendship, and companionship. Thus, we cannot rely solely on our feelings of love to anchor and sustain the relationship for the duration of the marriage.

In marriage, love and commitment are intertwined, and both essentials must coexist for the marriage to be successful. A successful marriage is grounded in commitment, "Until death (physical death) do us part."

Commitment is a conscious choice you make to act with integrity, respect, and care; even when you do not feel like it. Scott Stanley, relationship expert, describes commitment as "a dedicated choice to give up other competing choices." It is commitment that keeps the relationship together, whether you feel like staying in the marriage or not.

Commitment is what keeps the epic couple's relationship glued together during the rough patches and gets you through the long haul. A successful marriage is entirely dependent on the couple's commitment and the aid of the Holy Spirit to ensure its success. Without the aid of the Holy Spirit, commitment can become fickle and fleeting.

Commitment is evident in long-term marriages and is connected to the couple's emotional maturity. Your commitment is evidenced by the fact that you have chosen to be together, stick with each other, no matter what, for the long haul. Consequently, there is a willingness to love each other unconditionally and remain steadfast and committed, especially through the challenging times.

Commitment is something an individual has complete control over and can decide how it will be put into action. The scenario, My Life or My Wife?, is an excellent example of how commitment in marriage is put into action on a daily basis.

> **SCENARIO: My Life or My Wife?**
>
> After a long, hard day at work, the husband returns home to enjoy dinner with his family and is looking forward to his regular Thursday night pick-up basketball game at the local community center with friends. The husband is preparing to leave home when his wife informs him that she received a telephone call from her mother earlier that day. Her mother is coming to town for a brief overnight visit to attend a luncheon with former classmates the next day. The husband senses his wife is overwhelmed and has a lot on her plate in addition to needing to prepare the guest room for his mother-in-law. The husband decides to forego his game and stay home to support his wife to get through the household chores.

The husband has his own plans for the evening, but based on his strong commitment to his wife and marriage, he decides to forfeit his plans and support his wife to accommodate a last-minute visit from his mother-in-law. In this case, the husband demonstrates a key ingredient of commitment which involves making a self-sacrifice to support his wife at a time when she really needed it. Other indicators of commitment in marriage include acceptance, emotional support, calmness, respect, caring, kindness, friendship, and consideration.

Making a personal commitment to your spouse is reflective of the relationship between Jesus Christ and the church—His people.

According to Bishop Geoffrey Robinson, in his article on "Marriage as Covenant and Commitment," "marriage is a covenant relationship, and the language of covenant is a language of commitment." Bishop Robinson points out that, "Jesus committed Himself to the church of his followers and gave HIS life as an expression of His commitment. Similarly, the invitation to total commitment is inherent in the marriage relationship."

Making a personal commitment to your spouse is reflective of the relationship between Jesus Christ and the church—His people. This personal commitment is required to ensure that the promises under the marriage covenant will be maintained throughout the relationship and the temptation to operate outside the covenant relationship will be severely diminished.

In some secular circles, the idea of commitment raises a great deal of doubt and skepticism. Commitment is often associated with negative concepts such as being "tied down" or becoming "cut off" from engaging in "fun-filled" activities. Therefore, the thought of total commitment to another person becomes a source of tremendous anxiety and fear for some. This may trigger feelings of uncertainty because an individual does not know in advance what will be required of him/her during the course of the relationship. Ultimately, this can result in a lack of commitment all together or have severe consequences, such as relationship failure and family breakdown if the individual is already in a marriage.

Research by psychologist Joyce Webb, Ph.D., suggests that commitment is "the part of the relationship that provides safety and security, so couples can express their thoughts, feelings, and desires openly." Dr. Webb further notes that when couples are committed, they have greater confidence and reassurance they will survive the day-to-day challenges and stresses that can tear a marriage apart. In some sense, commitment acts like the glue, which forges a bond between the couple to support them to navigate their way through the rough patches.

Commitment for the epic marriage means loving when…

- The figure eight turns into the figure zero.
- When wrinkles become part of your daily life.
- The weight begins to pack on.
- His hair begins to recede, and a paunch develops.
- When everything begins to sag.
- When the physical profile begins to change.
- When he/she becomes sick.
- When physical sex is no longer possible because of illness.

The above list is only a tip of the iceberg that epic lovers' commitment overcomes. Let us examine some proven strategies that have helped many epic couples to strengthen their commitment to their marriages and see them strive and thrive.

Be Intentional About Making Your Marriage Work.
Epic couples who are committed to making their marriages work do not allow themselves to passively fall out of love. Instead, they act to ensure their relationship evolves into the next level. This takes prayer, dedication, and hard work. With the empowerment and guidance of the Holy Spirit, you may have to act in ways that are contrary to your feelings for the betterment of the marriage.

Continue to Manifest Loving Actions Even When Loving Feelings Are Not Present.
Committed married couples know that marriage has its seasons of "ups and downs." Committed couples have an uncanny awareness that they should continue to act lovingly toward each other even when the relationship is experiencing marital turbulence. Dr. Johnny C. Parker Jr., author of *Renovating Your Marriage Room by Room* says, "When a couple chooses loving actions, oftentimes loving feelings emerge again."

Set Goals for Yourselves.
Couples who set goals together have a common focus and work together, as a team, toward achieving their goals. Goals can help to provide direction for your marriage and strengthen your relationship, according to authors Carlos and Katherine Green of *The Family Goal Planning Guide and Workbook*. Setting spiritual goals can be a great way of increasing the commitment and bond between the couple.

Learn How to Love Each Other.
Take time to know your partner and identify his or her needs (know his or her love language as thoroughly discussed by Gary Smalley) and work toward fulfilling the partner's needs. In the *Five Love Languages*, understanding each other's love language is one of the keys to having lasting love, says Smalley.

Know How to Work Through Your Problems.
Listen to each other and commit to working through each problem and challenge as it arises. Remember to use the four pillars to a successful marriage which were previously identified—prayer; empowered, Spirit-led living; love; and service—to effectively communicate and work through difficulties. Committed couples who have sworn to commit to working together on addressing their marital and relational challenges will ultimately succeed until "death us do part."

A story was told of Dr. Robertson McQuilkin that exemplified an epic lover and marriage. It was a marriage that exemplified the above points of being intentional about making their marriage work until death. It expressed loving actions, even when loving feelings could not be reciprocated. They worked their life's goals together and learned how to love each other, and they worked through all their marriage challenges.

> Dr. McQuilkin once served as president of Columbia Bible College and Seminary (now called Columbia University) for more than 22 years. He resigned in 1990 to care full-time for his wife, Muriel, who suffered from Alzheimer's disease.
>
> Dr. McQuilkin met Muriel at the school when they were students. When they first met, he discovered

she was "delightful, smart, and gifted, and just a great lover of people and more fun than you can imagine."

Dr. McQuilkin married Muriel, and together they raised six children in 30 years of marriage. He and his wife served God in many ways, including 12 years as missionaries to Japan.

Muriel joined her husband on staff at Columbia; and in 1981, she was diagnosed with Alzheimer's disease.

In the initial years of the disease, Dr. McQuilkin tried to go to his office and fulfill his responsibilities at the school. But as soon as he left Muriel and went to the college, she would become anxious and distressed, sometimes even terror-stricken.

She would follow him to school; walking a half-mile to the school. She made that trip as many as 10 times a day. One time at night, he was helping her get ready for bed and noticed that she had bloody feet because she had walked so far to try to get close to him.

When speech began to fail Muriel, one of the last phrases Muriel could say was, "I love you."

In 1990, McQuilkin did something few married men would do. He knew the university and Muriel needed him 100 percent, so he resigned as president of the college to devote his time to care for his wife. McQuilkin wrote a letter to explain his decision to resign.

> *"It is clear to me that Muriel needs me now, full-time ... My decision was made, in a way, 42 years ago when I promised to care for Muriel 'in sickness and in health ... till death do us part.' So, as a man of my word, integrity has something to do with it. But so does fairness. She has cared for me fully and sacrificially all these years; if I cared for her for the next 40 years, I would not be out of her debt."*

> *"Duty, however, can be grim and stoic. But there is more: I love Muriel. She is a delight to me—her childlike dependence and confidence in me, her warm love, occasional flashes of that wit I used to relish so, her happy spirit, and her tough resilience in the face of her continual distressing frustration. I don't have to care for her; I get to! It is a high honor to care for such a wonderful person."*

So, Dr. McQuilkin became a homemaker and a caregiver to his wife, stepping into God's special assignment for him in this season of their lives.

Several times people would ask him if he ever got tired of caring for Muriel, to which replied, "No, I love to care for her..."

One special memory he recalled was Valentine's Day, 1995—he was riding an exercise bicycle at the foot of her bed and thinking of past Valentine's days, including the one in 1948 when he asked for her hand in marriage. Muriel woke up, smiled, and suddenly spoke for the first time in months: "Love … love … love," she said.

McQuilkin rushed over to give his wife a hug. "Honey, you really do love me, don't you?" he said.

In response came the words, "I'm nice"—this was her way of saying, "Yes."

Those were the last words she said aloud. Dr. McQuilkin continued to love Muriel until the end. By the time of their 50th wedding anniversary in 1999, she couldn't function on her own, and spent each day lying in bed.

Muriel's last day on this earth was September 19, 2003. In a letter to friends, McQuilkin wrote, "For 55 years, Muriel was flesh of my flesh, and bone of my bone. So, it is like a ripping of my flesh and deeper—my very bones," he said.

"But there is also profound gratitude. For ten years, I've delighted in recalling happy memories. I still do. No regrets. I'm grateful."

Many who know and do not know him would regard Dr. Robertson McQuilkin as one of the finest examples of "agape love." I do not consider him as a model of agape love, but more so a biblical model of a Spirit-filled lover who gave his wife all the love she ever needed—much more than agape love.

He loved her to the end. He made a promise and he honored his promise to Muriel. However, with the grace of God and the abiding presence of the Holy Spirit, he went on to live another few years with a new wife, Deborah Jones, a nursing professor, according to *Christianity Today*, whom he married in 2005. He continued to speak and write, in addition to serving as president emeritus of Columbia. He authored 19 books, including *A Promise Kept*, about the challenges he faced and life-lessons the Lord imparted in caring for Muriel.[1]

Dr. Robertson McQuilkin died and was buried June 4, 2016.

Dr. McQuilkin in life and death exemplified an epic lover. We too, can and should, live epic lives; so, at the end of our stories, our lives will reflect His story from birth, marriage, and death. Epic marriage couples live their lives knowing they have a promise to keep with each other and God. They are committed to enjoying their marriage and fulfilling all the blessings of God that marriage gives.

There are many people who would consider this story as unusual. Jenny and I find that this kind of marriage relationship is typical for epic lovers. Epic lovers make commitment with the promise to live with both the good and not so good times, "until death." It is not a novelty; it is a way of life and love. As you continue to read, understand that epic lovers practice on a daily basis, loving communication skills.

A Love Promise Worth Keeping

REVIEW QUESTIONS

1. Scott Stanley, relationship expert, describes commitment as "_____ _____." **Explain!**
   _____
   _____
   _____

2. Is it true that commitment is something an individual has complete control over and can decide how it will be put into action? Explain!
   _____
   _____
   _____

3. Fill in the blank. Commitment is "the part of the relationship that provides, _____, so couples can express their _____."

4. Fill in the blanks. Commitment acts like the _____ that forges a _____ between the couple to support them to navigate their way through the _____.

5. How did commitment make a difference in Dr. McQuilkin's story?
   _____
   _____
   _____

END NOTES

[1]Robertson McQuilkin has written about his life with Muriel in his book, *A Promise Kept* (Carol Stream, Illinois: Tyndale House Publishers, Inc., 1998).

ADDITIONAL READING SUGGESTIONS

Green, Carlos and Katherine. *The Family Goal Planning Guide and Workbook* (Power Couples Rock, LLC, 2017).

McQuilkin, Robertson. *A Promise Kept* (Carol Stream, Ill.: Tyndale House Publishers, Inc., 1998).

Parker, Johnny C., Jr. *Renovating Your Marriage Room by Room* (Chicago: Lift Every Voice, A Division of Moody Publishers, Inc., 2012).

Smalley, Gary. *Five Love Languages* (Chicago: Northfield Publishing, A Division of Moody Publishers, Inc., 1998).

CHAPTER 4

COMMUNICATING IN LOVE

It is commonly believed that the art of communication is the heart and soul of marriage—the better the communication; the healthier the marriage. Some people even liken it to the circulatory system of the body. Those who view communication as akin to the circulatory system subscribe to this theory, because the circulatory system consists of the heart and blood vessels that infuses blood through the entire body. It delivers nutrients and other essential materials to the cells and removes waste products. Without the circulatory system,

SCENARIO: Timing Is Everything

A busy working couple agreed to set time aside to discuss their decision to start a family. The husband asserts that now is the right time for them to embark on this great endeavor. The wife suggests that they may need to rethink this situation considering her recent promotion at work and postpone their plans for another year. The husband angrily points out that this matter has been continuously deferred year-after-year and there is no more room for delays because they are not getting any younger. The wife feels silenced and refrains from further participation in the conversation our bodies would starve to death. Likewise, communication is the lifeblood that supports, sustains, and keeps the marriage alive.

Couples living in epic marriages have learned how to become an expert in the correct methods and skills to effectively communicate in loving ways, unlike the scenario titled: Timing Is Everything.

There are many couples who are full of love and committed to their marriage, but have unhealthy communication skills, which are poisoning the lifeblood in their relationship. They are passionate and intimate, but they do not know how to share or express love in meaningful ways; and as a result, their marriage rides like a rollercoaster. Each person in the relationship has common goals and values, but there is a lack of cohesiveness between them. They all want to be loved and share love, but they lack the right communication skills.

Without proper communication skills and knowledge, the greatest marital dreams will never be realized. It is not only what couples say, but also how they say it, that can be the source of communication problems or joys in marriage. Effective communication is more than just exchanging information. It understands the words, emotions, body language, and the tone behind the information that is being transferred.

Conversely, communication failure occurs in marriage when one spouse feels that the other is not hearing, listening, or understanding their message. This communication blockage, can lead to frustrations, tensions, and arguments. In many relationships, the interest seems to be placed primarily in getting one's own point of view heard and understood rather than having an interest in hearing and understanding

Communicating in Love

of the other's point of view, according to Susan Brown, Licensed Clinical Social Worker (LCSW). A great deal of arguing could be avoided if couples would seek more to understand, rather than seeking to be understood.

When couples do not feel understood or affirmed, there is usually a strong emotional response which may take the form of silence, verbal outburst, or even physical violence. This usually results in feelings of frustration and can cause conflict, which can negatively impact the marriage relationship, as illustrated in the scenario example.

Experts in marriage communication agree that a couple's love life will get better if they are willing to learn effective communication skills. However, for many couples these techniques need to be learned to replace faulty practices and repair the marriage relationship.

> *Effective communication can facilitate therapeutic healing and renewal for couples who previously experienced communication challenges.*

Effective communication will enable couples to open up to each other and feel supported and validated; to work through problems and maintain a harmonious environment where caring and love can flourish. Effective communication can facilitate therapeutic healing and renewal for couples who previously experienced communication challenges.

Below are some key strategies that epic lovers have been using to ensure effective communication in their marriage.

Effective Listening:

"Wherefore, my beloved brethren, let every man be swift to hear, slow to speak, slow to wrath" (James 1:19 KJV).

Effective listening is an essential aspect of healthy communication. This involves more than just understanding the words or information being communicated, but also it includes the importance of understanding how the speaker feels and the emotions behind what is being communicated. Effective listening means we are actively engaged in seeking to understand the information that is being transferred to us.

Epic lovers understand the following principles: To be effective listeners, we must refrain from talking or interrupting. This is required to ensure that we are truly hearing and understanding the information that is being presented.

Tips for Effective Listening
1. *Focus fully on the speaker.* It is important to ensure that your attention is fully focused on the speaker. This is imperative in ensuring that you will not miss any nonverbal cues. Avoid anything that may distract you, including telephone calls, day dreaming, or thinking about something else.
2. *Avoid interrupting.* This has been said before, but it is important enough to reiterate again, because many of us tend to think ahead and finish the other person's sentence or jump in to get our own points across. This should be avoided at all costs, not only to demonstrate that you are focused on what is being said, but also that you value the opinion of others.

3. *Refrain from judgment.* People have a tendency to be judgmental of others. However, to be an effective listener, it is important to set aside judgment, blame, and criticism to fully understand the other person. This will help us to not make assumptions regarding their feelings or experiences.
4. *Show interest.* It is important to use nonverbal cues to show your interest and encourage the speaker to continue to share his or her experience. This may include expressions such as "yes" or "uh huh" to confirm your understanding. Your facial expressions and body posture should also be inviting and supportive.

The E-A-R Model

The E-A-R Model is a useful tool for effective listening and can be applied to any situation where effective communication is required. This simple model is a quick and easy reference to support enhanced listening:

E **Explore** using open-ended questions such as 'What" and "How" to ensure understanding and facilitate conversation. OBSERVE nonverbal cues.

A **Acknowledge** by paraphrasing what you think the message was.

R **Respond** appropriately.

As simple as this method might appear, it requires full attention and participation of the listener to master.

Nonverbal Communication

Nonverbal communication can include our facial expressions, body language, and gestures. These cues may also include our tone of voice, posture, muscle tension, and breathing, according to Jeanne Segal, Ph.D. and author, in her book, *Feeling Loved: Finding Happiness in an Overstressed World*.[1] Nonverbal cues are used in everyday communication, particularly when we are passionate concerning the things we care about. Understanding the use of nonverbal communication can support us to better gauge the feelings and experiences of others and enable us to express what we really mean.

The ability to read nonverbal communication can be easily developed through practice by observing people in various settings such as in a restaurant, bus, or train, as well as noticing how people interact and react to each other. It is important to notice how nonverbal communication differs among people with different life experiences, and we should take note of the different cues used, relating to culture, gender, and age, etc. For example, an African man, a teenager, and a grieving widow may use nonverbal signals very differently, according to Segal.[2]

> *When stress becomes overwhelming, it inhibits our capacity to self-monitor our communication approach that can cause us to overreact to the situation.*

In addition, it is equally important to note that nonverbal cues should be identified as a whole group, not as a single gesture. This is essential to ensure that we get a better overall sense of what the person is experiencing and not make leaping assumptions based on only a single factor.

Managing Stress

Stress can inhibit effective communication and can limit our ability to listen effectively while communicating. When stress becomes overwhelming, it inhibits our capacity to

Communicating in Love

self-monitor our communication approach that can cause us to overreact to the situation. This may result in your saying or doing something that you will later regret. Heightened stress may also cause the other person to react in a similar manner, which will hinder dialogue during the communication process. It is important to learn to quickly reduce stress in the moment, so you can return to a state of calm to effectively deal with the situation and determine the appropriate response required.

Tips for Dealing With Stress During Communication:
1. *Notice when you are becoming stressed.* Pay attention to what is happening to your body and how you are reacting in the situation. Your body will let you know if you are stressed and will exhibit symptoms such as tension in your jaw, clenched hands, a knot in your stomach, etc.
2. *Take a moment to calm down.* You can take a break or time out from the conversation and postpone it to a later date.
3. *Get in touch with your senses.* Taking a few deep breaths can be helpful and will assist you to return to a state of calm. Think of a soothing image in your mind that will also help you to relax.
4. *Look for the humor in the situation.* Find a way to lighten the mood. Humor, when used appropriately, can alleviate stress when you start taking things too seriously.
5. *Be willing to compromise.* Finding a happy middle ground can be a good way of de-escalating the situation and can help to enhance communication during the conversation. Compromise may be easier for you, particularly when dealing with issues that arise in the marriage relationship.

The EPIC MARRIAGE

6. *Agree to disagree.* Call a truce! Take a break from the situation so that you can calm down. Find a way to regain your balance by taking a walk or doing a quick meditation. This will recharge your batteries and assist you to continue the conversation.

Saying It Right the First Time

After couples learn listening skills, understand the nuances of nonverbal communication, and gain tools to minimize emotional stress in communication issues, they are now ready to plunge into basic principles of communication.

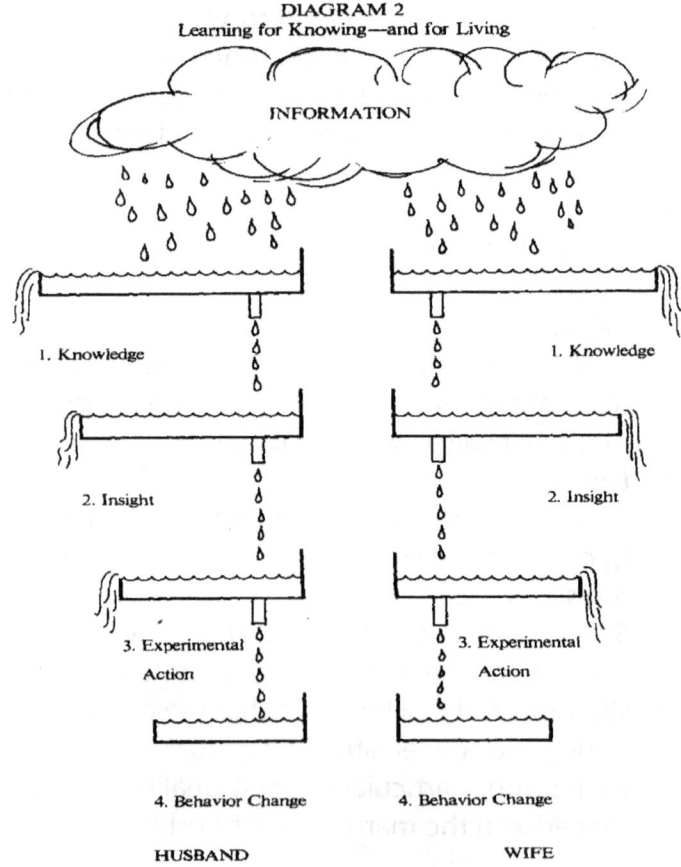

Dr. David Mace, one of the fathers of Marriage and Family Therapy, in his book, *Close Companion,* explained that in the communication process, all information must go through four successive processes before it has any real chance to influence marital behaviors. He explains the process in Diagram 2. [3]

The cloud in the upper level shows the information descending like raindrops on two troughs, which represent the minds of a couple. The information is collected like water in the troughs; but notice, it is only retained and processed at one end. At the other end, the trough is there as an opening where most of the accumulated information just pours away. Considerable amounts of information daily blitz husbands and wives, and nearly all of it makes a very shallow impact on their minds and is quickly forgotten. Dr. Mace says, some info remains and is processed as knowledge, which may be used in the relationship. This knowledge received is information systematically filed and ready to be used.

Dr. Mace further states,

> There is a small pipe in the base of the trough, which allows a few drops to fall into another less-extensive trough immediately beneath the first. This represents a very small amount of the information we receive, retain, and process as *knowledge,* some of which seeps down to a deeper level within us and becomes *insight*. This can be defined as knowledge that is especially relevant to our personal life situation, so that it is perceived by our inner awareness as offering us some advantage, such as a possible improvement in our marriage. At this point, however, no step has been taken to make use of the new knowledge. All that happens is that we entertain *a fantasy about what might happen if we acted on it.*[4]

The process continues as some of the insight gained trickles through the trough, and like the other troughs, at the open end, most of the insight pours away and is never acted upon. The trough also has a thin pipe through which a few precious drops penetrate to another still smaller trough beneath. This takes us to the third level, which is *experimental action*.

At the experimental level, change begins. The husband or wife sees and understands that there is something that can be done which might make his or her marriage happier and resolves to implement the change. Now let us look at how this process of change is fulfilled through the communication cycle.

Communication Cycle

Completing Your Communication Cycles. The first lesson in communication theory introduces couples to a three-step communication cycle.

In Step 1, Send verbal message—information

In Step 2, Repeat the knowledge that was verbalized, so that the sender may know the recipient heard the message; this is called "feedback."

In Step 3, The sender confirms the feedback, indicating whether the message is correct or wrong. If the feedback indicates a wrong interpretation, a clarification is given to the message.

The Communication Cycle

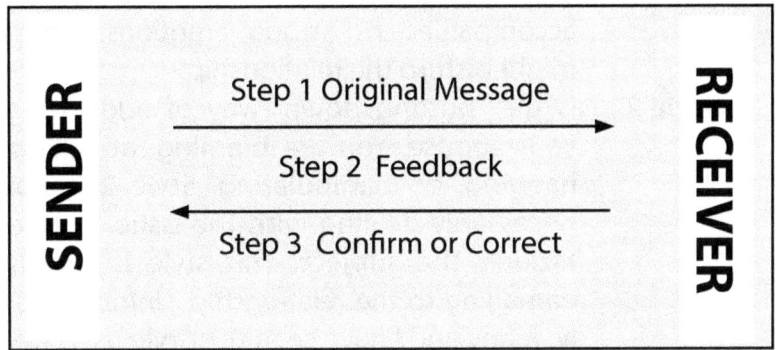

When couples learn this three-step process and use it in their relationship, it will have the potential to cause information to go through a process that can lead to aha moments, insights, and experimentation of the insight, which will lead to changes.

It is easy to learn this during a meal, while driving, or at leisure moments. Some couples may feel a tinge of self-consciousness at first when doing this. Some couples have said while trying this process that it makes them feel silly. However, after they have considered the value in the tool, and how useful it can be when crisis comes, they easily overcame their awkwardness and gave it a try.

I must state that this method is not the only communication tool. William Hill has four communication styles that have saved and prevented many marriages from ending in disaster. According to Hill, when couples communicate, they do so in one or more of four styles. As a married couple, you should be aware of the style you are using at any given time and learn to use the right one at the right time. What follows is a somewhat simplified description of Hill's models.

Style 1 . . . is simply passing on information or engaging in casual conversation. It is generally not accompanied by strong emotions, which might disturb the relationship.

Style 2 . . . is the "putting down" way of addressing your spouse. You are blaming, attacking, nagging, or manipulating. Style 2 is not necessarily dealing with the issue, but attacking the subject. This style is usually damaging to the relationship. Unfortunately, Jenny and I have seen this style used frequently with many causalities.

Style 3 . . . is an exploring, wondering, and speculative way of looking at a situation. This necessitates a coherent, investigative inquiry to see if the couples can understand what is going on between them and try to find a resolution. This model tries to minimize or ignore emotional pains and calls for an intellectual approach.

Style 4 . . . is a process of self-disclosure. Here a couple conveys where they are and what they are feeling, without blaming their partner or justifying self. One person may say, "I am feeling troubled and uncomfortable, and I need your help to adjust or change these feelings."[5]

The aforementioned communication models are discussed as examples which epic lovers have at their disposal. One style, however, does not fit all. Whether a couple uses the Air, Mace, Communication Cycle, or Hill model, epic lovers are guided first and foremost by the leading and guidance of the Holy Spirit to choose the appropriate method that will facilitate the best result.

Communicating in Love

Emotional Awareness and Communication

As we close this section, we feel it would not be wise to end the chapter only speaking about the methods or techniques of communication. One of the major challenges in couple's communication styles is learning how to handle emotional pain, or angry feelings. Some couples choose to deny or ignore their feelings. Others use their emotions and anger to motivate them to act wisely for resolutions. And some use their emotions and anger as fuel for their communication. Couples should be aware that their attitude reveals a great deal through their body language. And, one of the most powerful barometers of communication is wordless nonverbal cues. We communicate more through nonverbal than verbal communication.

When couples are upset, words alone rarely convey the issues and needs at the heart of the problem. During a discussion, we may listen for what is felt, as well as what is said. We pay close attention to the other person's nonverbal signals, which may help us to figure out what they are really saying. Our ability to accurately read another person depends on our own emotional awareness. The more a spouse is aware of his/her own emotions, the easier it will be for the mate to pick up on wordless clues that reveal what he or she may be thinking and feeling.

> *Our ability to accurately read another person depends on our own emotional awareness.*

Epic lovers have a healthy, emotional safety net which allows them to have a great communication system to help preserve their oneness and uniqueness. They feel safe to be vulnerable, knowing that their lover's response will not be defensive or judgmental. Epic lovers maintain a healthy communication structure to provide for one another's growth individually and corporately. Structure means they will agree upon certain rules of communication to handle their conversations and keep them from escalating out of hand. Why? They know their love will only grow and intensify throughout the years, because of their deep desire to love and nurture one another through the artful use of communication skills.

Because of what you have learned and will master in communication skills, know that you have now opened the doors to all the other benefits of marriage and family lives. As you integrate these fundamentals and are being guided by the Spirit, family praxis of prayer, love, and service, epic lovers could learn how to break through impasses and bring more gratification in the communication dynamics.

If the circulatory system of the body is communicating correctly, it will provide all the other systems of the body with all the essential nutrients required for optimum functionality. Likewise, when communication is working well in marriage, it provides the necessary elements to facilitate the health and well-being of the marriage. The right communication skills, guided by the Holy Spirit and administered in loving ways, help couples to create a diamond- and/or pearl-like relationship out of their marital challenges.

Communicating in Love

REVIEW QUESTIONS

1. Fill in the blank. Effective communication understands the words, _____ _____ _____ behind the information that is being transferred.

2. Is it true that effective communication can facilitate therapeutic healing and renewal for couples? Please explain!
   _____
   _____
   _____

3. What are the effects of talking or interrupting a speaker in the communication process?
   _____
   _____
   _____

4. According to Mace, what happens at the "experimental action stage"?
   _____
   _____
   _____

5. Should a listener take into account what is "said and felt" when replying to a speaker? Explain your answer.
   _____
   _____
   _____

END NOTES

[1] Jeanne Segal, *Feeling Loved: Finding Happiness in an Overstressed World*, Helpguide.org International, 2014.
[2] Segal, Ibid.
[3] David Mace, *Close Companions* (New York: Continuum, 1982).
[4] Mace, Ibid.
[5] William Hill, found in Robert C. Berg, Landreth, and Fall, *Counseling Concepts and Procedures*, (Abindom, U.K., 2013).

CHAPTER 5

DIAMOND LOVE: CREATIVE USE OF CONFLICT

Think back to the very first time you met your spouse, and if it was love at first sight, reflect on what you thought caused the attraction. You were so captivated and fascinated with everything he/she was, that you were not only excited to see and spend quality time with each other, but you also looked forward to hearing every word that came out of your new lover's mouth. Your lover saw you as a flawless illustration of the woman described in Proverbs: "She speaks with wisdom, and faithful instruction is on her tongue" (31:26 NIV). You, as a female, saw your lover, "radiant and ruddy, outstanding among ten thousand" (Song of Solomon 5:10 NIV).

For the guy, his lover was not only intelligent but also beautiful. She was nearly perfect. As far as you were concerned, there was nothing she could do or say to get an angry reaction out of you. You had finally met your perfect helpmate, your soulmate. You married the love of your life. The above descriptions are common experiences of our Western love relationships.

Now, fast forward a few years: One ordinary evening when you are winding down after dinner, suddenly, an innocuous comment swiftly shifts that tranquil mood into a firestorm. You notice that lately this conflicted pattern seems to be happening repeatedly. You are acutely aware of the scathing, bitter words exchanged during the conflict. You begin to ask yourself how you got to this uncomfortable place of disagreement and dissatisfaction. You begin to wonder how you can have this unsavory situation return to what it was before.

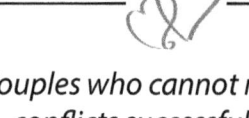

Couples who cannot manage conflicts successfully are doomed either to settle for a relatively unsatisfactory marital relationship characterized by "ups and downs," or drift gradually into separation that mocks the dream of a loving, intimate marriage.

In marriage, conflicts are inevitable and come about because of "a clash of wishes," as defined by Folsom. However, we find out that differences only cause major trouble when the people concerned are intimately related to each other. Two people, who should cooperate with each other, suddenly find themselves in disagreement and are in trouble. Unless they can either disengage from each other or find a solution acceptable to both, there will be a head-on collision—"clash of wishes."

In other words, conflict is rooted in *difference*.[1] A conflict is a disagreement *heated-up*.[2] A disagreement is a difference accentuated by lack of personal space. So, there are two factors always present when conflict develops—the wishes are different and personal space is limited.

Couples who cannot manage conflicts successfully are doomed either to settle for a relatively unsatisfactory marital relationship characterized by "ups and downs," or drift gradually into separation that mocks the dream of a loving, intimate marriage.

Think of a verbal disagreement between a couple when one person says "yes," but the other says "no." The couple may desire to talk to each other and clear everything up, but they cannot find the right opportunity or the time to have that conversation. When a series of unresolved conflicts build up over time, it can put a tremendous strain on the relationship. This tendency has the capacity to set the marital ship adrift, resulting in confusion, dissatisfaction, and uncertainties.

Married couples often experience different types of conflicts during the course of their marriage. Money and financial matters can be a main source of marital conflict as described in the scenario example. Couples often have different ideas regarding money management. It is important prior to marriage that couples know the values and feelings they have related to money before it becomes a massive headache in the years ahead.

Preparing a budget and planning for expenses usually requires negotiation and compromise. Epic lovers should set money, financial priorities, and goals for their future to minimize undue conflicts. Some couples may react to the conflict described in the scenario in a variety of ways. Among them are the following:

Avoid It. Everyone's first reaction to an impending collision is avoidance. Many couples choose this route indirectly to address differences in marriage. This method seeks to maintain a superficial state of peace which involves sidestepping every potential quarrel and sweeping all disagreements under the rug. This method inevitably creates a phony relationship. An example of avoidance based on the scenario posited previously is as follows:

Tolerate It. Many couples simply shrug their shoulders in resignation. They are prepared to accept the *status quo* believing that periodic quarrels are an inevitable part of marriage, that nothing can be done to alter this reality, and that the only courses to follow are to bear with the unpleasantness, make up later, and enjoy a period of relative tranquility until the next quarrel breaks out. The result is a relationship with alternating phases of harmony and disharmony, what we often speak of as the "ups and downs" of married life. Using the scenario presented above, the husband may react to the situation in the manner described below:

> **Money Matters**
> The husband identifies the wife's purchase of a new pair of shoes when reviewing the bank statement and brings it to her attention. From her response, he realizes that this issue could easily escalate and turn into a conflict situation. The husband quickly changes his tone and jokingly says that they will need to build a bigger closet to make sure there is enough room for all her shoes.
>
> The husband identifies the wife's purchase of a new pair of shoes when reviewing the bank statement. He is both angry and disappointed but does not share his feelings about this with his wife. The husband concludes that his wife is irresponsible and has no idea regarding how to properly manage money.

Fight Fair. This is the doctrine widely promulgated by George Bach that fighting in marriage is okay, but it should be done in accordance with prescribed rules learned by taking a course in "fair-fight training." "Fair fighting is a conflict-resolution process; it is a set of rules designed to help couples discuss their differences within boundaries, and in this way preserving the relationship over the need to "win over" the other."[3] We have met couples who said they found this helpful, and others who have been unable to make it work. To me, Daniel, fighting in a love relationship seems totally inappropriate when we think about the success of the marriages built on the foundation of Christian values.

Spirit-filled Marriage and Family. This method of handling conflict does not rely on avoidance, tolerance, fight-fair only, or simply maintaining *homeostasis*. The secret to a successful marriage is built on the following elements:

1. **Prayer**
2. **Empowered, Spirit-filled Living**
3. **Love**
4. **Service**

Let us examine how this approach can be used to address the conflict situation identified in the "Money Matters" scenario described earlier, from the perspective of the husband:

Perspective of the Husband

Prayer	Holy Ghost-Empowered Living
The husband prays about the situation and his concerns and asks God for wisdom and guidance to effectively address it.	Through the gentle guidance of the Holy Spirit, the husband will raise his concerns with his wife in a spirit of meekness.
Love	**Service**
The husband displays a spirit of empathy as he actively listens to his wife's response to identify areas of mutual interest to solve the problem.	The husband responds lovingly in helping his wife bring a mutual agreement to the matter.

Similarly, the wife upon hearing the concerns identified by her husband will use a similar approach to processing and responding to the issues raised:

Perspective of the Wife

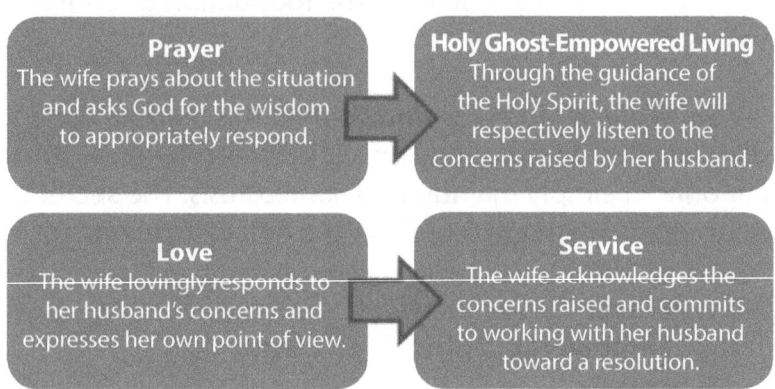

Couples often wonder why it is there are so many tension-related issues that lead to conflict. The answer is, a spouse feels safe and comfortable enough to act or speak in a way without filtering thoughts, tones, or feelings. Whereas with other people, they tend to be coolheaded, thoughtful, and watchful of their words. It is fine for couples to feel comfortable and safe with each other, but the Spirit-filled marriage seeks not only to speak freely but also to speak in love guided by the Holy Spirit to minimize conflict. And if and when conflict comes, they pray for the Spirit's guidance as to what method of approach to use, and in love, couples seek to resolve the conflict for the betterment of the marriage relationship.

Using Conflict Creatively

> "Hatred stirs up conflict, but love covers all wrongs"
> (Proverbs 10:12 NIV).

Diamond Love: Creative Use of Conflict

The art of conflict resolution is not simple. What you learn in the outside world is either to fight and win, or if you *cannot* win, how to exploit the resulting situation to placate your adversary and get the best deal possible. Marriage is not a competitive sport, in which winning or losing is considered relevant. In a loving marriage, it is the joint interest that is the main goal.

The "Blessed With Children" scenario highlights the challenging and rewarding task of raising God-fearing children. This requires a great deal of focus and energy from a couple. Husbands and wives often hold opposing and sometimes conflicting views concerning parenting. These individualized parental norms are usually influenced by the parental method experienced within their respective families of origin. It is important for parents to present a united front on rules and decisions made when parenting. Otherwise, children will learn how to play one parent against the other to get what they want. This situation can significantly contribute to further conflict in the marriage if left unresolved.

> **SCENARIO: Blessed With Children**
>
> A couple has three children and their eldest daughter, now 13 years old, is just entering her teenage years. Recently, she has become very interested in socializing with her friends and was invited to the movies. The husband does not have a problem with his daughter going out with her friends, but the wife believes she is still a little too young to be going out without adult accompaniment. This difference of opinion has resulted in a serious disagreement between the two which has resulted in a great deal of tension in the home. The wife has asserted that the husband's laid-back approach to parenting their children requires an immediate intervention.

Conflicts can be productive, but it is essential to understand conflict resolution strategies to ensure disagreements do not become destructive. We can use conflicts to benefit the relationship if we learn how to handle them competently.

Dealing with conflict requires three distinct steps:

1. The couple must clearly understand the true nature of conflict. What is happening in this scenario is that one of the negative areas of difference related to the couple's conflicting view regarding how to parent their children is asserting itself and needs to be closely examined and resolved. This is at least how a conflict *starts*. However, if it is not faced as it arises, the conflict can expand and pull in a whole set of other differences that have not been previously cleared up. It is as if you said to your partner, "I don't agree with your thinking regarding this matter, and I'm angry about it. And, while I am at it, let me add that there are several other things you do that I don't like either."

This piling up of unhealed injuries from the past can be terribly destructive and unproductive. There is only one way to avoid it, and that is to *take the conflicts one at a time and work through each one.*

2. The anger must be taken out of the conflict before it can be effectively resolved. The anger emotion is perfectly healthy and legitimate when appropriately expressed. Anger can be useful to signal to your spouse that you are extremely unhappy with the current situation. Anger is a surge of power that can enable each individual to break through the impasse and get his or her own way; however, this is not the ultimate goal when attempting to work through marital conflict.

Diamond Love: Creative Use of Conflict

> "A hot-tempered person stirs up conflict,
> but the one who is patient calms a quarrel"
> (Proverbs 15:18 NIV).

Anger creates a crisis, because when couples are angry, they cannot love; and when they love, they cannot be angry—the two emotional states exclude each other. What couples need is the ability to understand and accept each partner's position; but the capacity to do this is usually inhibited by the heated emotions surging. Couples cannot, while the anger lasts, identify with the other person, or concede the validity of his or her point of view. They cannot even hear accurately and fairly, what he or she is saying.

Anger paralyzes and temporarily suspends the capacity to act cooperatively. Until we can take the anger out of the conflict and focus on the disagreement that caused it, we will not be able to negotiate a solution. The anger must first be controlled, and the energy be directed to conflict resolution.

3. A mutually acceptable settlement of the underlying disagreement must be negotiated. It is only when the anger has been processed that any negotiation can be undertaken. A disagreement does not have to heat up into a conflict before it can be dealt with. And if some heat *has* developed, it need not be sustained. The conflict previously mentioned in the "Blessed With Children" scenario outlined above can be immediately resolved using the approach which was highlighted in the first chapter of this book.

Here is a closer look at how the key principles which form the foundation of a successful, Spirit-filled marriage and family can be applied in this case:

Dealing with the Conflict as a Couple

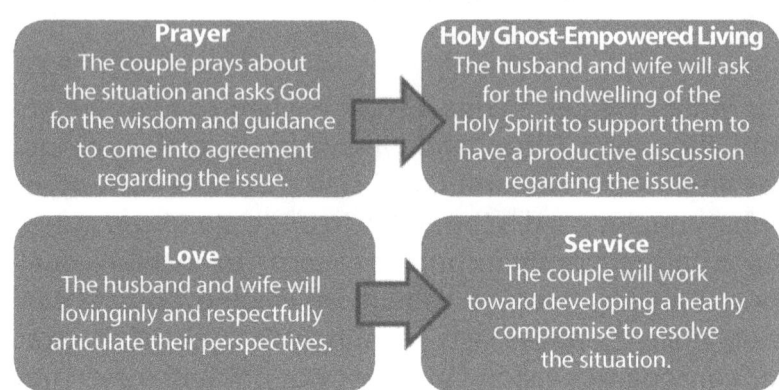

Few couples have learned much about the use of negotiating skills or about the strategies that are available to them to effectively resolve conflicts. Let us take a more in-depth look at conflict.

Overcoming the Conflict Iceberg

Couples living in a Spirit-filled marriage always choose to address conflicts before they form an Iceberg. The following figure outlines what constitutes most conflicts. Over the years, Jenny and I have noted that the smallest problems are always magnified to become the core issue in most marital conflicts. If we can self-identify the ninety percent of the so-called iceberg submerged under the surface of the water, such as the unresolved issues from the

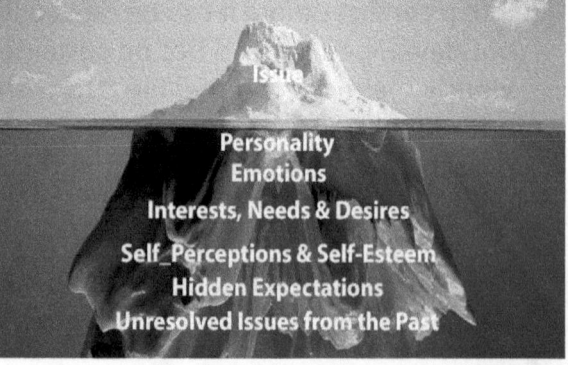

past; hidden expectations; self-perceptions and self-esteem; interests, needs, and desires; emotions; and personality, they are able to address the issues to be resolved. Epic lovers who choose to learn how to communicate the iceberg issues will help to put the conflict issues into perspective.

Role of Communication

The topic of communication has been dealt with more extensively in Chapter 4 of this book which is titled, "Communicating in Love." Communication plays a significant role in conflict resolution. During a conflict, it is essential that we listen effectively and use words and phrases that lead to a collaborative effect. This approach will ensure that there is not an escalation in an already difficult situation.

Our attitude is reflected in the use of both verbal and body language. The most important methods of communication are wordless. When people are upset, words rarely convey the issues and needs at the heart of the problem. During a conflict, we listen for what is felt, as well as what is said. We pay close attention to the other person's non-verbal signals, which may help us figure out what they are really saying. Our ability to accurately read another person depends on our own emotional awareness. The more we are aware of our own emotions, the easier it will be for us to pick up on wordless clues from our spouse that reveal what they may be thinking and feeling.

Emotional Awareness and Conflict

Emotional awareness refers to the consciousness of your moment-to-moment emotional experience and the ability to manage all your feelings appropriately. Emotional awareness is the basis of a strong communication process. It allows us to take responsibility for our contribution to the conflict and corresponding resolution. Emotional awareness helps us to understand and control the internal chatter that leads to an escalation of anger, contempt, and hostility.

Our reactions can be controlled and changed when we learn to watch for cues within ourselves that surface when we become irritated. For example, more rapid breathing or change in our voice tone. Because of paying attention to these cues, we can develop and implement measures and techniques that work for us and will allow us to shift our responses and reactions. This will ultimately assist us in controlling the conflict. Strategies such as deep breathing and visualization can be introduced when there is an escalation in the situation. This will enable us to reduce the emotion and energy attached to our manner of communication.

Emotional awareness helps us to understand and control the internal chatter that leads to an escalation of anger, contempt, and hostility.

Emotional awareness enables us to better understand ourselves, including what is really troubling us and to communicate issues clearly and effectively. A high level of emotional awareness also helps us to understand what is troubling other people and allows us to stay motivated to address the conflict until it is resolved. Epic lovers allow themselves to become sensitive to one's emotional awareness levels. In the spirit of compassion, they seek to reach out to avert or manage conflict to bring about resolution.

While conflicts are inevitable in the marriage, they present unique opportunities for personal growth and enhanced communication between the couple. Each conflict allows the couple to develop a better understanding of themselves, both individually and corporately. Conflicts

Diamond Love: Creative Use of Conflict

have the potential to strengthen and deepen the intimacy in the relationship as long as there is a commitment to ensure that conflicts are resolved swiftly and intentionally as they arise.

The ability to collaboratively address the conflicts and challenges in the marital relationship will indeed strengthen the bond between the couple and result in a continual appreciation for each other. It will help create a dazzling, diamond-looking relationship of which others can only dream.

There is a general belief in culture that says, women are fascinated with diamonds, hence the cliché, "Diamonds are a girl's best friend." Men, on the other hand, will do all they can to win and sustain women's love. They are willing to go out of their way to work hard and make sacrifices to purchase these precious jewels for their wives. Epic lovers receive pleasure when they see their wives looking happy and feeling good among their peers, and if diamonds make them feel more special, giving diamonds will be their goal.

Conflicts, when properly handled, have the potential to turn one's marriage from an ordinary black charcoal into one of the finest, clearest, cleanest-cut and radiant diamond relationships one will ever see.

Truly, diamonds are one of the best ways to express love for someone special. The next time when you venture into a jewelry store and admire an incredible diamond ring or when you look at the diamond ring you are wearing; just think about the time, energy, and resources that went into its making. You will surely have a better appreciation for it.

In like manner, we must remember that a diamond is the hardest substance that exists on the planet. It requires great pressure to produce it, and so does a good marriage.

Conflicts, when properly handled, have the potential to turn one's marriage from an ordinary black charcoal into one of the finest, clearest, cleanest-cut and radiant diamond relationships one will ever see. Getting this beautiful diamond-type marriage requires ridding the relationship of blemishes, resulting in better clarity. The cuts in diamonds enhance the color and shine, as well as hiding inclusions. We discover also that if the cuts of diamonds are too deep or too shallow, the diamond will not have a good dispersion. According to gemologists, some diamonds are handled improperly, and as such, they resemble a synthetic diamond, but nothing can compare to the real thing.

When married couples constantly try to avoid, tolerate, or fight out their conflicts, they have the potential to keep their marriage at an inexpensive charcoal level. On the other hand, when married couples humble themselves and allow the Holy Spirit the opportunity to use conflicts in the marriage to work for the marital good, it will help to produce a rare diamond or pearl-type marriage that would be the envy of other married couples.

A pearl is formed inside an oyster when a foreign substance slips into the oyster. The substance irritates the mantle. The oyster responds by covering the irritant to protect itself. Over time that covering creates a pearl of great value. Whether it is foreign matter that enters the relationship or natural daily matters that disturb a marriage, homeostasis—the way epic lovers handle these matters—will create an expensive treasure that enhances their marriage union for their lifetime.

As we travel the world conducting relationship and marriage conferences and seminars, one of the most frequent statements we have heard from many couples is, "we would like to have a loving marriage like yours." Our response has always been: "It is possible, but only if you choose to properly deal with all your conflicts and allow the Holy Spirit to use each conflict to show forth His glory in you."

We must go on the record as saying, "Our marriage is not better than any other," we have chosen to allow our conflicts to build the character of Christ in us, and it is a daily effort. Every conflict is still painful. But we are committed to allowing God to use these conflicts for His glory in us.

So, when you reflect on the initial feelings of love and romance you had for your mate during the early stages of your relationship, you should marvel at your continuous success in sustaining lasting joy and happiness. Epic love grows and intensifies throughout the years as a result of the couple's deep desire to love and nurture one another with the aid of the Holy Spirit, as well as their commitment to using the artful resolution of conflict to bring out the diamond- or pearl-like love life that adds joy in their marital journey.

REVIEW QUESTIONS

1. What is the root cause of conflict?

2. What is conflict?

3. How does conflict help an epic lover?

4. What are a few things that cause an iceberg conflict?

5. What role does emotional awareness play in conflict management?

END NOTES

[1]Difference refers to "not seeing eye-to-eye or not having the same understanding."
[2]Heated-up refers to "growing more animated or combative."
[3]https://en.wikipedia.org/wiki/Fair_fighting

The EPIC MARRIAGE

CHAPTER 6

JOYFUL OR HAPPY LOVERS

Our wedding day was one of the happiest days of our lives. The day we had spent most of our earlier years dreaming of had finally come and all the stress associated with wedding planning and preparation seemed to have evaporated. When I saw my beautiful wife, Jenny, walking down the aisle and singing the song, "Ave-Maria," my heart was filled and overflowing with such rapturous joy that I found it difficult to contain my emotions. I felt happy when the minister said: "Sir, you may now kiss your bride." We were finally married and will be together till death parts us. For me, Daniel, there would be no more lonely days. I would always have someone to share my life, love, and my joy with.

Most men, like me, got married with a high dose of happiness and joy . . . enough, they believed would keep them for the rest of their married lives. We were always expecting to live and nurture a relationship filled with joy and happiness. Oh, what a dream! If only that could be a reality! The world would have less stress, divorce, and sickness, but more peace and prosperity.

Dr. Gary Thomas in his classic, *Sacred Marriage*, grabbed the attention of observers in the subheading, when he questioned the concept of happiness in marriage: He asked, "What If God Designed Marriage to Make Us Holy More Than to Make Us Happy?"[1] I believe this question was designed by the writer, not only to capture the imagination of his readers, but also to see marriage through different perceptual lenses. Focus on holiness before happiness. Why would he lead his reader that way?

According to an article published by *Science and Technology*'s point of view, "The Science of Happiness" (March 20, 2018), it reports Dr. Acacia Parks is an assistant professor of psychology at Hiram College, where she teaches on the "science of happiness," and contends "happiness is a combination of how satisfied you are with your life (for example, finding meaning in your work) and how good you feel on a day-to-day basis . . . our general happiness is more genetically determined than anything else."[2] The social scientists who have been studying positive psychology for more than 40 years have concluded there are three major sources contributing to happiness: genes, events, and values.

> *Since happiness is fueled by circumstances, and circumstances change frequently, marriage should not be viewed as grounded happiness.*

Happiness is based on circumstances. Since happiness is fueled by circumstances, and circumstances change frequently, marriage should not be viewed as grounded happiness. For hundreds of years immemorial, couples have been chasing the illusive game of happiness with the hope of keeping their marriages alive and healthy. Not even King Solomon in the Bible could find and keep happiness. He concluded: "All is vanity and vexation of spirit" (Ecclesiastes 1:14 KJV). Epic couples realize that it is futile to try to control their circumstances and the flow of events

Joyful or Happy Lovers

in their lives; likewise, it would be counterproductive to plan or pursue happiness which is fleeting. Instead, epic-couple marriages choose to pursue joy.

Epic couples are aware that happiness and joy can be present at the same time, but they are two different emotions. Happiness is based on external things or events. Therefore, if things happen to go well, you are happy, but if things go awry, then your happiness is likely to disappear because it is circumstantial.

Another truth that couples need to understand is this—the Bible never promises happiness; it only promises joy. You can have joy and be happy or sad, but you cannot really be happy without joy. It is not wrong for couples to seek happiness in their marriage; the only problem is, it is temporary.

> *Epic couples are aware that happiness and joy can be present at the same time, but they are two different emotions.*

Judith Wallerstein and Sandra Blakeslee in their book, *The Good Marriage,* posits a list on how people define a happy marriage. Their findings were gleaned from their exhaustive research and interviews of successful couples across America. Consider the list below:

1. Respect between the partners
2. Each person cherishes the other
3. Each person likes the other
4. Each finds pleasure and comfort in the other's company
5. Emotional support of each other
6. Mutually satisfying physical intimacy
7. Expression of appreciation between the partners
8. The creation of fond memories
9. A feeling of safety, friendship, and trust

10. A feeling that the spouse is central to his or her world
11. An admiration of positive qualities such as honesty, generosity, decency, loyalty, and fairness
12. A strong sense of morality
13. The conviction that each person is worthy of being loved
14. A sense of reality, in that there are some problems but that they are surmountable
15. A view that each partner is special in some important regard
16. A sense that the marriage enhances each partner
17. The sense that there is a unique fit between each partner's needs and the spouse's willingness and ability to meet those needs
18. The sense that each partner is lucky to have the other
19. An equitable division of household tasks and childrearing
20. A sense that the success of the marriage is attributable to both partners
21. An ability to express both positive and negative emotions
22. A shared view that the marriage takes constant attention and work[3]

Wallerstein and Blakeslee's work outlines the things that combines to create happiness, but epic couples know they need more than the above list to keep their marriages joyful. They are aware that when sickness, death, loss of job, birth of children, or any serious challenges arise, more often than not, happiness disappears, and it is only joy that keeps them safe and sane in the crucible of life's most demanding challenges.

Joyful or Happy Lovers

The Science of Joy

Joy, unlike happiness, is not all about *me*—joy is connection. Beethoven was believed to have little happiness, but he knew joy. He linked joy to a connection with a power greater than himself.

Social scientists who study happiness and joy, say happiness activates the sympathetic nervous system (which stimulates the "flight or fight" response); whereas, joy stimulates the parasympathetic nervous system (controlling "rest and digest" functions). Social sciences say, "We can laugh from either joy or happiness." Vaillant said: "We weep only from grief or joy." Happiness displaces pain, but joy embraces it: "Without the pain of farewell, there is no joy of reunion," he asserted. "Without the pain of captivity, we don't experience the joy of freedom."

happiness is a place to visit, not a place for epic lovers to live.

Yet there is far more research on happiness than on joy, the "least-studied emotion," according to Vaillant, whose next book's working title is, *Faith, Hope, and Joy: The Neurobiology of Positive Emotion. He says,* "For the last 20 years, emotion has been an unwelcome guest at the table of scholarship." He continues, "We treat joy as secret, dirty, and awful, the way the Victorians treated sex. Happiness is largely cognitive; it is a state of mind, not an emotion. That's why social scientists and economists love to study happiness. Happiness is tame."[4]

Epic married couples understand that happiness is a noun, and it is not something that they own. The truth is happiness is a place to visit, not a place for epic lovers to live.

Scripture's View of Joy and Stress

The word joy appears 88 times in 22 of the Old Testament books; 57 times in 18 of the New Testament books. On the other hand, the Bible does not specifically use the word *stress*; however, it speaks about anxiety, worry, and trouble. These emotions tend to lead to stress because believers fail to trust God to provide the necessities of their lives.

Looking at joy, the Psalms are filled with references to joy. Example: "Weeping may tarry for the night, but joy comes with the morning" (Psalm 30:5b NIV), and "Shout for joy to God, all the earth" (Psalm 66:1 NIV). In the New Testament, we are told that joy is a fruit of the Holy Spirit (Galatians 5:22), which means that it is a Christian virtue. All Spirit-filled Christians should have this virtue (fruit). Given this biblical emphasis, we need to know and understand what joy is and pursue it in our marriages.

It is both a Christian's duty and moral obligation, to be joyful. Consequently, the failure of a Christian to be joyful is sinful. Where there is unhappiness and the absence of joy in the life of a believer, it is the clearest indication that the flesh is operational.

Of course, there are times when as Christian couples we all experience sorrow and disappointments. It is perfectly legitimate to mourn when we experience, sorrow, grief, and loss; these feelings are not sinful in and of themselves.

Biblical joy is not removed when one is mourning, suffering, or undergoing difficult circumstances. They go hand in hand. The person mourning is experiencing grief, but in the same moment, he/she possesses a measure of joy, because

> *Stressful thinking leads to stressful feelings and both have the tendency to deplete our joy.*

joy is not measured or determined by circumstances. It is not transient, but fixed. Why? It is a gift of the Holy Spirit. Yes, it is possible to have joy in every sphere of human experience, because it is sourced in the Holy Spirit.

For a Spirit-filled believer, the starting point for dealing with stress is Jesus Christ. He offers believers encouragement to deal with stress when He says: "Let not your hearts be troubled. . . . Believe in God; believe also in me" (John 14:1). Believing leads to trusting. Proverbs 3:5-6 asks us to, "Trust in the Lord with all your heart, and do not lean on your own understanding. In all your ways acknowledge him, and he will make straight your paths" (ESV). Finally, the last scripture and maybe the best Scripture passage to capture on how to handle stress is, Philippians 4:6-7:

> Do not be anxious about anything, but in everything by prayer and supplication with thanksgiving let your requests be made known to God. And the peace of God, which surpasses all understanding, will guard your hearts and your minds in Christ Jesus (ESV).

Stressful thinking leads to stressful feelings and both have the tendency to deplete our joy. Christian couples choosing to master stress and live a joy-filled life, need to know what stress is.

Stress is defined as "our body's response to the demands that we place on it." Those demands may be spiritual, physical, mental, or emotional in nature, and when we place these demands on our bodies, medical science tells us chemicals and hormones, such as cortisol and neuropeptides, are released into our bloodstreams and then we *feel* stressed.

Stress by itself is neither good nor bad. It is indeed a normal part of life, so we can never escape it altogether. What really matters is how we deal with it and that will determine whether the effect will be negative or positive. Every married couple experiences and deals with stress differently, because, there is no one-size-fits-all stress treatment. However, for epic couples, the cure is sourced in the Word of God.

Epic couples realize that stress not only impacts their joy, but it also has the capacity to impact and affect their health in negative ways if they do not manage it correctly.

The American Academy of Family Physicians reports that two-thirds of all doctor visits are due to stress-related ailments. It is also believed that 80 to 90 percent of all diseases are stress-related.[5]

According to researchers, laughter releases endorphins into the body that act as natural stress busters.[6] And medical science explains that, a good belly laugh gives our heart muscles a good workout; improves circulation; fills our lungs with oxygen-rich air; clears our respiratory passages; stimulates alertness hormones; helps relieve pain; and counteracts fear, anger, and depression—all of which are linked to illnesses. Epic lovers filled with happiness and joy will always incorporate laughter as a medicine to their bodies and souls.

Joy Enlightens

Webster's dictionary defines *joy* as:

(1) To experience great pleasure or delight: Rejoice,

(2) The emotion evoked by well-being, success, or good fortune, or by the prospect of possessing what one desires: Delight.

Joyful or Happy Lovers

Joy is a state of mind and an orientation of the heart that is released by God. It is a settled state of serenity, assurance, and hopefulness.

Kay Warren, the cofounder of Saddleback Church with her husband, Rick Warren, in Lake Forest, California, in her devotional book, *Choose Joy: Because Happiness Isn't Enough*, defines *joy* as: "Joy is the settled assurance that God is in control of all the details of my life, the quiet confidence that ultimately everything is going to be all right, and the determined choice to praise God in every situation."[7]

Chase After Joy

Joy is a fruit of the Spirit. It is supernaturally produced in our hearts. It comes in abundance when couples totally depend on God who is central in their hearts and minds. Joy is based on the confidence couples have in Jesus Christ.

Just because couples are smiling, does not mean that their marriage is conflict free and all is going well. They may not be experiencing happiness, but, their confidence is in the Lord, and they can count

SCENARIO: Show Me Some Love

After a long day at work, the wife returns home to begin making dinner for the family that evening. She is exhausted but acutely aware of the need to get through several additional household chores, including laundry and preparing the children's lunches for school the next day, before winding down for the evening. Her husband comes into the kitchen and barely acknowledges her as he breezes by on his way to the home office. The wife thinks about how nice it would have been for her husband to greet her with a warm hug and a big kiss and take a few minutes to chat with her to find out how she is doing before moving on to his next activity.

on Him, for even in the midst of their trials they can experience "pure joy."

The scenario, "Show Me Some Love," could be repeated over and over in many marriages. Any ordinary Christian wife would be feeling unloved and possibly upset. Her desire for affirmation which was unmet could have shut down her emotions and negatively positioned her into a state of sadness that evening. This expectation could set the tone for the evening and could have lasted a long time if it had not been addressed.

A Spirit-filled wife's approach to the seeming rejection could be, to quietly pray and make her petition known to God instead of attacking her husband for not meeting her expectation. As she prays, the Holy Spirit fills her heart with love, and reveals to her the stress her husband had at work; so, she took a break from her chores in the kitchen and reached out to her husband. There in the office, he told her about an unfinished project that he had to turn in before bed. She gave him time to finish his project, and he joined her to put the children to bed. They both went to bed feeling love and joy in their hearts. The wife chose to chase after joy, rather than allowing sad feelings to steal her joy.

> ...happiness is like a thermometer that rises and falls with the circumstances. It reacts and is "controlled" by environment.

The Spirit-filled Christian couple's home is different from a religious or secular home because it is controlled by the Holy Spirit. The command: *"Be filled with the Holy Spirit"* simply means to be controlled by the Holy Spirit (Ephesians 5:18). It is an ongoing process, allowing the Holy Spirit to control you. What fills you controls you!

Joyful or Happy Lovers

Christian couples that are controlled by the Spirit of God are joyful persons, not necessarily happy persons. (Ephesians 5:19). This kind of joy does not rise and fall with good experiences or bad experiences. It is not dependent on external circumstances, but it stems from a confidence that God is in control and that is enough for her, in good or bad situations. It is a steady, abiding joy.

Someone says happiness is like a thermometer that rises and falls with the circumstances. It reacts and is "controlled" by environment. On the other hand, joy is like a thermostat, it sets the climate. Joy changes the marital climate instead of being controlled by it. Epic couples seek joy daily!

The apostle Paul tells us how he remained joyful, even in prison: "I have learned that in whatsoever state I am in, therewith to be content" (Philippians 4:11 KJV). He was happy with what God ordained for his life.

Likewise, for couples living the epic-married life, accept what God brings your way with joy, knowing that it is for your good.

The Immovable Joy

We have joy because we have Christ, His Word, and the indwelling presence of the Holy Spirit. The apostle Paul writes: "May the God of hope fill you with all joy and peace in believing, so that by the power of the Holy Spirit you may abound in hope" (Romans 15:13 ESV).

Biblical joy does not depart when couples suffer lost and shed tears. Paul made it clear that they both can coexist, as he writes: "As I remember your tears, I long to see you, that I may be filled with joy" (2 Timothy 1:4 ESV). This illustration shows that both joy and tears can coexist as Paul exhibited the longing to see Timothy again and wept over him with a joyful heart. Furthermore, James exhorts the church to, "Count it all joy, my brothers, when you meet trials of various kinds" (James 1:2 ESV).

For Spirit-filled Christian couples, joy is an attitude of the heart and spirit. It is present inside them as an untapped reservoir or prospect.

The epic-married couples see joy as that which is recited in some of the old black spiritual songs: "This joy that I have, the world didn't give it to me. The world didn't give it, and the world can't take it away." This too is the mantra of all epic couples. The Old Testament prophet Nehemiah, reminded his workforce that "the joy of the Lord is your strength" (Nehemiah 8:10), as they dealt with opposition to their building project.

> *Choosing joy helps epic couples find true meaning, happiness, and fulfillment where it matters most—in their relationships with their families, especially with one's spouse.*

Epic Lovers Always Choose Joy

Choosing joy brings a measure of peace, comfort, and purpose to your life in ways you may not currently recognize are possible. Choosing joy helps you slow down and soak up every beautiful moment that life should offer.

Choosing joy in marriage does not mean epic couples' lives will be perfect; but it does mean that they will be able to see and recognize perfect moments in their journey and give thanks and praise to God for them. Choosing joy helps epic couples find true meaning, happiness, and fulfillment where it matters most—in their relationships with their families, especially with one's spouse.

Spirit-filled couples know that their circumstances tend to create happiness, but it is their attitude that will create joy. There are many biblical references that combine bad experiences and joy together.

1. Our hearts ache, but we always have joy. We are poor, but we give spiritual riches to others. We own nothing, and yet we have everything (see 2 Corinthians 6:10).
2. . . . despite severe suffering, you welcomed the message with the joy given by the Holy Spirit (see 1 Thessalonians 1:6).
3. Dear brothers and sisters, when troubles come your way, consider it an opportunity for great joy (see James 1:2).

Spirit-filled Christian couples should always find reasons to be joyful in all circumstances. Joy is something that is deep within and does not leave quickly. When we have the joy of the Lord, we will know it and so will others. Since joy is given by God, and it is a virtue He wants us to have, we need to be joyful!

In addition to being joyful, according to the Church of Christ book titled, *Believe*, chapter 22 on Joy says, "We should let others have their joy and not bring them down when they are excited about good things. The only thing worse than not having joy, is stealing someone else's joy."

Reading the Scriptures will bring us joy! "And these things we write to you that your joy may be full" (1 John 1:4).

If Christian couples cannot find reasons to be joyful in their relationship, their perspective must change. They need a refilling of the Holy Spirit. Paul writing to the Ephesians commanded them "to be filled with the Spirit" (Ephesians 5:18). After being filled with the Spirit, they began to sing songs—hymns—to God and give thanks (vv. 19, 20).

God lets couples have blessings every day. We should be able to see them and thank God for them.

Many couples believe they should be filled automatically with joy. No... It is not an automatic filling. It is something you can ask for, "You do not have because you do not ask" (James 4:2 NIV). When you are feeling low, ask God to increase your joy. Ask for joy!

How Can Couples Rejoice Always?

The apostle Paul speaks repeatedly about joy and about the Christian's duty to rejoice in his letter to the Philippians: "Rejoice in the Lord always" (4:4a). Paul's message is clear, Christians are to rejoice always—not sometimes, periodically, or occasionally—then for emphasis, he adds, "Again I will say, rejoice" (v. 4b). Paul had one of the greatest challenges of his life. Paul wrote this epistle from prison, and in it he addresses very gloomy matters, such as the possibility that he will be killed (martyred), poured out as a sacrifice (2:17). Yet, he tells the Philippian believers that they should rejoice, notwithstanding his condition.

Here, the apostle was making it clear to Christians, whether married or single, that being joyful is a matter of discipline or of the will. How is it possible to remain joyful all the time? Paul gives us the key: "Rejoice *in the Lord always.*" The key to the Christian's joy is its source, which is the Lord. If Christ is in me and I am in Him, that relationship is not a sometimes experience. The Christian is always in the Lord and the Lord is always in the Christian, and that is always a reason for joy.

Even if the epic couples cannot rejoice in their circumstances when they find themselves passing through pain, sorrow, or grief, they still can rejoice in Christ.

Joyful or Happy Lovers

Even if the epic couples cannot rejoice in their circumstances when they find themselves passing through pain, sorrow, or grief, they still can rejoice in Christ. They rejoice in the Lord, because He never leaves them or forsakes them; they can rejoice always.

Rejoicing does not remove the negative circumstances, but it refocuses couples' energy in the right direction.

Emma Seppala, Ph.D. in her book, *The Happiness Track*, reports research done by Shelley Gable and Jonathan Haidt, suggesting that people have three times more positive experiences than negative ones in their lives. That being the case, what's causing them to focus on the bad ones? Researchers answer this question, telling us they have identified two main predispositions that keep people from experiencing, extending, and expanding their joy, they are negatively biased and conditioned.[8]

How can Christian couples change these tendencies and focus more on the positive experiences in their lives? The answer comes in another study done by Nathaniel Lambert and colleagues at Brigham Young University; they contend that discussing positive experiences leads to heightened well-being, increased overall life-satisfaction, and even more energy.[9] Simply put: more joy. A better biblical answer would be, do like Joshua and Caleb. They chose to give a positive report in the face of multiple negative reports (Numbers 23), telling Israel that with God's help they could take the Promised Land.

While happiness is determined by circumstances, joy is a state of mind or a state of being. As a married couple, you could be encountering the worst of situations in your life and still have joy, because circumstances do not determine it. One of the mistakes couples make when they contemplate marriage is to believe that once they are married their spouse will make them happy. This is a fallacy, no one can make you happy, and it is unfair to foist that burden on anyone. No one can make you happy; they can only contribute to your happiness. If the individuals were not happy before marriage, soon they will learn that one's spouse cannot make them happy if they themselves were not happy.

Epic couples understand there is no easy way to navigate life's journey without ups and downs. Many epic couples view married life to be like a roller coaster, but they know that the attitude displayed in the ride is what will determine the outcome. Epic couples know that married life is not a smooth road. But they know that they are not alone in the journey. They know they have the indwelling Spirit with them. They trust in the Word of God and are committed to enjoying the ride by keeping their joy alive as they trust and rely upon Jesus Christ. Epic lovers ride the roller coaster of married life with confidence, knowing that they can look forward to their daily doses of joys and sharing the gift of intimacy that can only be found totally and fully in the open relationship between each other.

Joyful or Happy Lovers

REVIEW QUESTIONS

1. Explain the difference between happiness and joy.
   _____
   _____
   _____

2. How is joy received?
   _____
   _____
   _____

3. How does an epic lover maintain joy in the marriage?
   _____
   _____
   _____

4. What are two roadblocks of joy?
   _____
   _____
   _____

5. Fill in the blank. Happiness is determined by _____ and joy is _____.

END NOTES

[1] Gary Thomas, *Sacred Marriage*. (Grand Rapids: Zondervan, 2015).

[2] The Science of Happiness, https://www.scitecpov.com/blog/2018/1/22/the-impact-of-public-funded-rd-on-economic-growth-zy9ea

[3] Judith Wallerstein and Sandra Blakeslee, *The Good Marriage* (Brentwood, TN: Grand Central Publishers, 1996). The author posits a list of how people define a happy marriage.

[4] George E. Vaillant, *Faith, Hope, and Joy: The Neurobiology of Positive Emotion* [not yet published].

[5] Susan Smith Jones, Ph.D., article, "More Joy, Less Stress in Eight Easy Steps," originally appeared in the May/June 2009 issue of *Unity Magazine*®. Reducing stress is important; we've all heard it. Stress not only impacts your happiness, but also your health. The American Academy of Family Physicians reports two-thirds of all doctor visits are due to stress-related ailments. It's also believed that 80 to 90 percent of all diseases are stress-related. And if you're female, stress may be even more damaging to your health. Study after study has found that women suffer from both stress and depression more often than men.

[6] Social laughter releases endorphins in the brain, says University of Turku, June 1, 2017. https://www.sciencedaily.com/releases/2017/06/170601124121.htm

[7] Kay Warren, *Choose Joy: Because Happiness Isn't Enough* (Grand Rapids: Revell, 2012).

[8] Shelly Gable and Jonathan Haidt, found in Emma Seppala, *The Hapiness Track* (New York: Harper Collins, 2016).

[9] Nathaniel Lambert, Ph.D., Professor at Brigham Young University.

ADDITIONAL READING SUGGESTIONS

Seppala, Emma. *The Happiness Track* (San Francisco: HarperOne, 2017).

Thomas, Gary. *Sacred Marriage* (Grand Rapids: Zondervan, 2015).

Warren, Kay. *Choose Joy: Because Happiness Isn't Enough* (Ada, MI: Revell, A Division of Baker Books, 2013).

The EPIC MARRIAGE

CHAPTER 7

THE FEARLESS LOVER
(MACHO SEXUAL FULFILLMENT)

A woman visited my friend, who is a follower of Christ, in a medical doctor's office, and this is a summary of her story as he reported it to me!

> "Doc," she said, "I have a problem with my husband! We have been married 15 years, and we are having a bit of problem behind the bedroom door."
>
> "What problem?" The doctor asked.
>
> "Doc, we're getting a little older; he's 41 and I'm 35, but he's giving out on me. We used to have sex all the time in all hours of the night, in all rooms in the house. Well, in the past eight months my husband has changed."
>
> "Tell me how he has changed."
>
> "He is not satisfying me much anymore. During sexual intercourse, he is unable to maintain an erection as he did before."

"He says, 'it's too good' so that's why he can't last, but I know he is having problems keeping it up even though he hasn't officially admitted it."

The doctor interjected and said, "That is a problem that can be easily fixed."

The woman continued, "I'm in the best shape I've ever been in my life, but he does not work out. I know if he starts to work out, he would last a little longer."

The doctor said, "You seem to be educated about sex."

She replied, "Yes, I read a lot, so I can please my husband."

She took a pause and then continued...

"Doc, I know he's not seeing anybody else because he comes home the same time every night. I need him to fix this or I'm going to shut it off."

The doctor saw the desperation in her face.

He replied, "That would not be good."

She interrupted him and asked, "How do I remedy this situation?"

We begin this chapter with this story, which was told to me (Daniel) by a friend who gave me permission to retell it.

The Fearless Lover

According to my friend, this story is a common occurrence in his office. What is not clear in the story was the faith belief system of the woman. However, what is crystal clear is, she believed her husband had a sexual problem, and she wanted him to get help and get it soon!

In this and the following chapter, Jenny and I will be discussing sexuality issues as they are viewed through the eyes of the sexes. We neither claim to be experts, nor claim to possess a medical degree. We want to present you with enough information that will help you the reader to be the best epic lover you can be. And that requires a balanced view of spirituality and sexuality. Jenny and I would like to say that we too have had many similar stories like the one at the beginning of the chapter during our counseling experiences.

Most of the counseling we provided through the years is focused on premarital, martial, and family counseling. We have had a limited amount of day-to-day counseling on sexual issues because the subject of sex and sexually related issues are generally off-limits or taboo among Christian couples, until there are problems in the bedroom.

Oftentimes, when these intimate issues are raised in counseling, there is a tendency to be evasive, on the part of the counselees, choosing to treat it as a secondary issue. Many Christian couples, particularly Christian husbands, are afraid to openly discuss, admit, or confess there are problems, particularly of a sexual nature in their marriage.

We are providing the following discussion to help husbands know God cares about their sexuality and sex life as much as He cares for any other area of their lives. So, we begin with one of the first and biggest challenges that many husbands face, ED (erectile dysfunction).

Men need to be informed and become aware that erectile dysfunction ED, is not the result of sin or necessarily a disease; in many cases, ED is a sexual dysfunction. Researching ED has revealed that it is a common problem among men of all ages. The good news is help is available. We will return to this issue later in the chapter.

Many couples, especially Christian husbands, tend to avoid any serious discussions on sex and tend to suffer in silence, as a consequence of their inability to intentionally address the problem head on. Ironically, the same men who are reluctant to seek professional help with their sexual dysfunction, according to research, are men who almost obsessively think about sex more than women. If it is true—men are obsessed with sex—why is there an apparent reluctance to seek professional help? Taboo keeps them in bondage!

Jenny and I are happy to know there is an increasing cultural shift concerning sexual norms within our churches. The church is becoming more open to discussing the subject, and the taboos once associated with the subject are diminishing with the increase in information and awareness.

Listen to what Steve Harvey says in his book, *Act Like a Lady, Think Like a Man*. Harvey contends that there are three things that men want in a marriage, they are, "love, support, and the cookie!" So, let us make it clear from the start—men love sex, aka, "the cookie!"[1] Talk to most married women, and they too would agree that their husbands love sex.

Men and Sex

Men cannot help but love sex. According to Edward O. Laumann, Ph.D., a professor of sociology at the University of Chicago and lead author of a major survey on sexual practices—The Social Organization of Sexuality: Sexual Practices in the United States—the majority of adult men under the age of 60 think about sex at least once a day, but only about one-quarter of women report this same level of frequency. As men and women age, each fantasize less, but men still fantasize about it twice as often.[2]

No wonder Solomon admonished men in poetic prose to develop ways and use their thoughts and minds to appreciate their wives. In Proverbs 5:19, he wrote: "Let her be as the loving hind and pleasant roe; let her breasts satisfy thee at all times; and be thou ravished always with her love" (KJV).

Yes! Be intoxicated with her love! Notwithstanding, this acid truth is one of the biggest problems husbands face in their marital journey—learning how to channel their sexual desires and love in wholesome and healthy ways. For too long, Christian husbands have chosen to ignore this problem and/or choose to deal with it on their own.

> *The issues of love and sex are too complicated and cannot be dealt with simply by utilizing one's personal resources.*

The issues of love and sex are too complicated and cannot be dealt with simply by utilizing one's personal resources. If husbands are expecting to have healthy, loving sex lives, they need solid guidance and therapeutic intervention through Christian counseling and the Word of God. Men need to disabuse themselves of this faulty notion which says, seeking help is something shameful or conspiratorial, in the sense that it undermines their manhood. They find it easy to secure the services of a lawyer for legal problems, accountants to address financial problems, and spiritual leaders for spiritual problems; but when it comes to sexual problems, they are reluctant to consult their doctors, counselors, or therapists. It is time to "man up," brothers!

Erectile Dysfunction (ED) is not your fault. Stop blaming yourself. Live your best life today, seek help, and follow the principle of Matthew 7:7-8, which says, "Ask, and it will be given to you; seek, and you will find; knock, and it will be opened to you. For everyone who asks receives; he who seeks finds; and to him who knocks, it will be opened."

Sexual Challenges

Many Christian husbands choose to deal with their ED problems through the spiritual disciplines of prayer and fasting. Prayer, fasting, and the use of Scripture are very helpful tools, but the issues of love and sex usually require more than prayer, fasting, and Scripture. We cannot negate the power of prayer, fasting, and other spiritual disciplines in relationships. However, they are not the only cures! God approves and uses medical science and medical professionals to apply medicine and medical procedures to heal the body.

Let us consider this as believers. We prayed and fasted for the right partners; we prayed throughout the period of courtship and premarital counseling for guidance; we prayed for the wedding; and we prayed for a happy and fulfilled marriage. Jenny and I submit to you that if our loving marriage is to continue to remain robust and healthy, we must continue to utilize all the spiritual disciplines deemed necessary for its continuity. But that will not be enough.

Within the Christian community, you will discover a plethora of testimonies concerning the power of prayer and the guidance of the Holy Spirit in undergirding husbands in their sexual struggles. If a man spends serious quality time praying for the indwelling presence of the Holy Spirit to fill up his life, He will give him the ability not only to have a sexually fulfilled life, but also a spiritually disciplined life.

Sex not only includes physical, emotional, and mental dimensions, but also it includes a spiritual dimension. All spiritual dimensions require the empowerment of the Holy Spirit. So, the question is, "Do you want to have the best sex life possible?" Share your sexual issues in prayer. Include prayer in your relationship.

Take time to pray together daily. Prayer will help built the kind of intimacy that is so needed to create the best sex life. It will create the level of intimacy that will lead you to share your sexual issues with your partner and, if needed, with other resource individuals that can provide the resources to having a better love and sex life.

I want to quickly note that once you have prayed, the Holy Spirit will guide you into all truths in handling the issues of love and sex, which might also require some education and attitudinal change. Once education is acquired and there is a change in attitude, you are now ready to take your love and sex act to another level.

Well, I have prayed, fasted, and used scripture, but our love and sex life are still mediocre and routine, as well as going downhill. I have heard many husbands say to me, "I really love my wife and she does feel the same about me. But, why are we still struggling sexually?" or "We are very actively involved in our church. We have a fairly decent life. What else can we do to improve our love and sex life?" Well, I am glad when these questions are asked, because the core problem in these situations is usually not sex; the problem is, many couples, mostly husbands, do not understand their sexuality development. The sooner they do, they will be better able to maximize the gifts of love and sex to their fullest potential.

> *Love and sex are experienced differently at different stages in marriage.*

Love and sex are experienced differently at different stages in marriage. Why, you may ask? Because love and sex changes in marriage. Love and sex are not static; they are a dynamic duo. They change over time and function differently in the various stages in marriage.

In my second book on *Love Factor in Marriage,* chapter 9, "Keeping Love Alive in the Stages of Marriage," I have discussed the five stages in marriage. In this chapter, I demonstrated that love and sex are viewed differently at the honeymoon stage because of the high levels of romance and love chemicals washing the brains of the new lovers. However, at the transformational stage where couples have matured and grown into a more cohesive oneness, love and sex involve a great deal more mental happiness and physical satisfaction.[3]

It is important for married men to first find out what stage of marriage they are in, and then evaluate their sexual struggles accordingly. Too many husbands are struggling with sexual issues that are hindering their marital growth and development when there is help and assistance available to them. Issues such as, masturbation, pornography, oversaturated sex drives, low libido, premature ejaculation, and erectile dysfunction, contribute to their predicament. Irrespective of how difficult and complex they may appear to be, they can be corrected. Did I hear a reader ask, "How?" Glad, you asked!

The first thing you need to do is decide that you will seek professional help. Most of these problems were not self-induced or self-inflicted; most of them may have been caused by life changes; such as the kind of food you eat, lack of exercise, age, medication, and stress, just to name a few. There is always help available. If you choose to continue refusing help, you and your spouse will continue to live unfulfilled lives. When men refuse to get help for their sexual issues, it not only affects them personally but also their entire family—wife, child, etc.

Getting the much-needed help for your sexual problem will not only improve your love and sex lives, but also it will enable husbands to live longer and healthier lives. Now, let us look at another of the major sexual issues facing married men.

Erectile Dysfunction

What is erectile dysfunction? ED is when a man has difficulty "getting it up," that is, to have and sustain an erection that will enable him to engage in sexual intercourse that is equally satisfying and fulfilling to both him and his partner. ED was once called impotence. Today, nearly all men who seek treatment receive some measure of relief. Some men may be saying they do not have ED because they have erections while they are sleeping, or they wake up with one. Medical research shows some men with ED will still have erections while they sleep.

Medical science has now determined that ED can occur at any age.

This is usually a sign their ED is not physical, but psychological—usually stress or depression. On the other hand, if you do not have nighttime erections, that usually means your ED has a physical cause.

What Causes Erectile Dysfunction?

Erectile dysfunctions are caused primarily by blockage of blood flow to the penis. It could be vascular in the sense that a faulty vein allows blood to drain too quickly from the penis. And yes, there are other physical disorders, as well as hormonal imbalances and certain operations that may also result in erectile dysfunction.

In the past, the medical community viewed psychological problems and aging as causal to erectile dysfunction. Medical science has now determined that ED can occur at any age, although it is more common in men older than 75. As men get older, it takes a longer time for arousal; urologists credit physical factors as responsible for triggering the majority of erectile dysfunctions in men over age 50.

It is reported that ED problems among younger men are generally caused by psychological problems. Their ED may come from tension and anxiety that may arise from poor communication with the spouse or a difference in sexual preferences. Medical science tells us their sexual difficulties may also be linked to the following factors:

- Stress
- Depression
- Fatigue
- Feelings of inadequacy
- Personal sexual fears
- Rejection by parents or peers
- Sexual abuse in childhood

On the other hand, medical research reveals there are many general causes to ED, but some of the major sources are:

- Diabetes (high blood sugar)
- Hypertension (high blood pressure)
- Atherosclerosis (hardening of the arteries)
- Alcohol and tobacco use
- Some prescription medications, such as antidepressants, pain medicine, and medicine for high blood pressure
- Low testosterone levels, etc.

Feelings That Can Lead to Erectile Dysfunction

Literature tells us that some ED problems are caused by both medical and psychological reasons. Many men experiencing this can trace their problems to feelings of nervousness concerning sex, perhaps because of a bad experience or because of a previous episode of temporary impotence. Other ED episodes are caused by feelings of stress, like work stress, family situations, church, or sickness.

It could also be depression or self-consciousness that you cannot enjoy sex or thinking that your partner is reacting negatively to you. These feelings throw water on the sexual fire. Sex is not just physical; it is also psychological, emotional, and mental. The most powerful sex organ is the brain. Therefore, the use of negative feelings lowers one's sex drive.

Is Erectile Dysfunction Just Part of Old Age?

No! Erectile dysfunction does not have to be part of getting older, it happens to all men. The main difference with having sex when you are old is, sex for older men requires more stimulation (such as stroking and touching) to get an erection, and it will require more time between erections to have sex.

Older men should still be able to gain an erection and enjoy sex. Growing older doesn't mean giving up sex; even men in their 90s can be sexually active.

ED and Sex Drive

Sex drive tends to go down in men with ED. However, please note, if you are not as interested in sex as you used to be, your testosterone levels might be low, and you may need a blood test to find out. ED is not synonymous with Low T (testosterone). Most men with ED do not have Low T, but if you do, that is probably the cause of your ED. If you have Low T, it is not the end! See your doctor to get medical help.

Medical research reveals that ED can be a sign that you are at risk with other health problems: heart disease, stroke, high blood pressure, or diabetes. A narrowing and hardening of your arteries, the same disease that causes heart attacks and strokes, can cut off blood supply to the penis. Do not ascribe any disease to yourself because of your ED. I am sharing this just so you can see your doctor and take all necessary precautions to protect your intimacy and potentially save your life.

How Is Erectile Dysfunction Treated?
Medical research tells us there are various methods in treating ED. One of the most effective approaches is injection, but the medical community states that it is the least preferred choice. That works for 80 percent to 90 percent of men; however, it does not hurt as much as it might sound. Most men say the injection feels like a pinch.

Other medical treatment options are medications such as: Cialis, Levitra, Viagra, and a natural treatment, vigor, along with natural herbal remedies. None of these medications or herbs will provide an erection on their own without arousal. It is reported that these medications generally help seven out of ten men with their ED. Men with ED often try these first because they are easy to use.

What Other Options Do I Have?
We have addressed a few of the issues with ED; however, you can do much on your own to help correct or control ED. Commit to change your lifestyle by losing excess weight, increasing physical activity, eating healthier, getting adequate sleep, rest, and exercise. Seek professional help to design lifestyle changes and provide a system to

monitor your changes. There are other treatments, but we will leave those discussions for our readers' medical practitioners, sex therapists, or urologists.

We have spent a good amount of time addressing ED but not masturbation, pornography, oversaturated sex drives, low libido, and premature ejaculation. This is not to belittle the importance of these other issues, on the contrary. From our research, these other issues will be addressed in some form when an ED patient seeks spiritual and profession help.

The Choice to Know

From all we have seen in Scripture, we are convinced it is God's will for couples to have loving marriages and to be fully and mutually satisfied sexually (see 1 Corinthians 7:3-5). Sexual happiness is not a one-sided pleasure. The husband's sexual happiness must include the sexual satisfaction of the wife. When husbands function as epic lovers, they become more motivated in seeking to satisfy their wives sexually over against their own desires.

> *We need to know that God created men and women to express love and sex differently.*

It is believed that more husbands find sexual joy and fulfillment when their wives are sexually satisfied. So, how can epic lovers know that they are satisfying their wives sexual needs? By simply committing to study, know, and understand their wives' specific moods, emotions, hormonal issues, her sexual triggers, and other relational desires and sexual conditions.

If husbands are going to become experts in their sexual relationship in their marriages, there are some things they need to know about their wives in order to fully enjoy and appreciate this wonderful gift of God.

As husbands, we need to know that God created men and women to express love and sex differently. The differences are designed to lead couples to learn about each other, so they can serve the needs and build the oneness needed for a successful marriage. It is only when husbands intentionally invest time to understand the differences between their wives and themselves are they able to communicate the kind of love that is needed to produce the right quality sex. The same approach is applied to the wives. But we will address that in the chapter on women, love, and sex.

Epic loving husbands who commit themselves to learn about the differences and meanings of love and sex between men and women, particularly their own wives, will gain the necessary knowledge, skills, and tools to master their love and sex relationships. Richard Sine wrote an article published in *WebMD* titled, "Sex Drive: How Do Men and Women Compare?" In it, he listed seven patterns of men and women's sex drives which researchers have found.

He says:

a) "Adult men under 60 think about sex at least once a day and only about one-quarter of women say they think about it that frequently.
b) Men seek sex more avidly than women.
c) Women's sexual turn-ons are more complicated than men's.
d) Women's sex drives are more influenced by social and cultural factors. Men have every incentive to have sex to pass along their genetic material.
e) Men and women travel slightly different paths to arrive at sexual desire. Women want to 'talk first, connect first, and then have sex.' Sex is the connection for men.

f) Women experience orgasms differently from men. Men, on average, take four minutes from the point of entry until ejaculation, according to Laumann. Women usually take around 10 to 11 minutes to reach orgasm, if they do.
g) Women's libidos seem to be less responsive to drugs. Men have embraced drugs as a cure not only for erectile dysfunction but also for a shrinking libido."[4]

As much as Richard Sine did not write from a Christian worldview, it is important to note the points outlined, which highlight the general differences between men and women with or without faith. What is the purpose of the above report? It tells us, the readers, that husbands and wives view love and sex differently—psychologically, physically, emotionally, and spiritually.

Psychologically, men are turned on by what they see; whereas, women are turned on by connectedness. It is also described by psychologists that men connect and feel loved through sex, whereas, women generally desire sex as the consequence of feeling loved and connected. They are turned on sexually through validation. A wife is validated by her husband's sexual interest if that is expressed through connection and affirmation, rather than through the pursuit or expression of need.

Generally, men often wonder why there is a difference in women's sexual needs. The first answer is biological. Everything about the man's sexuality is on the outside. The eye is the gate to the man's sexuality; whereas, everything about the woman's sexuality is on the inside. The emotion is the gate to a woman's sexuality. It is easier stimulating men, because his sexual organ is regulated by a different temperature system. Not so with the woman, whose sexuality is regulated by the normal body temperature system, mood, and health conditions. There is more work on the body to adjust and provide for the sexual excitement and stimulation for the wife.

Another major difference between the sexes is that when it comes to having sex, men just want a place and women want reasons, a mood, and a cause. Consider this: a man will go with a woman in the back of his car with ease; whereas, the woman, if prepared properly, may go anywhere with her man. Now this might sound a bit risqué, but the point being made is simply that if the woman's emotional needs are attended to, there is no telling what she will do with the love of her life.

> *Couples who daily connect spiritually, socially, psychologically, and physically will have more frequent and enjoyable sex.*

Another major hurdle men must overcome is the combination of male constancy and the ever-changing, complex femininity of women. Navigating the minefield of these two extremes and having the potential to keep sex alive in marriage is realistic, but it requires hard work.

Couples who daily connect spiritually, socially, psychologically, and physically will have more frequent and enjoyable sex. So, men, let us think about this. The more you pray together, call, or text, or brush against your wife, the greater each desire will grow. Oxytocin is released through touch. Allow the chemistry to flow through the body by letting her know that she is still desired, irrespective of the age. Through the act of touching, the husband affirms his wife that her body is still desirable and that each time you can, you cannot avoid a touch. What a great feeling this gives to a woman, to be always wanted by her man. So, epic loving brothers, work at the touching and the timing games, the dividends can be mind-altering. Once again, with the education that you will gain through reading this book, the guidance of the Holy Spirit, and practicing loving actions, you are going to get this right.

It is true that many husbands suffer sexually because they expect their wives to function on their sexual timing. This kind of expectation creates sexual stress and frustration. To minimize sexual frustrations, husbands need to know and understand their wives, and seek to satisfy them. In doing so, their needs will be met with less pain and frustration. The key to a wonderful and blissful sexual experience in marriage is for men to sacrifice their needs; and since a man's need for connection is not felt like a woman's, it is best for him to go her way. Going her way will make the sexual experiences more pleasurable and rewarding for both.

Finally, brother, we would like to let you know that your wife functions sexually on two tracks at a time. An epic lover will always focus on achieving both physical arousal and emotional readiness before he proceeds to intercourse. Her body may be ready for intercourse, but emotionally she is not receptive. Physically, the woman has a great deal that must happen to her body before she is ready to proceed. More important, the woman must experience emotional satisfaction. This bonding, meshing, blending, and connecting with her husband must happen first before she can feel comfortable and relaxed enough for the sexual encounter.

He delighted in every aspect of her very being, personhood, and her sexuality.

Let us observe King Solomon and his love relationship with the Shulamite woman. Solomon wooed the Shulamite through what we call the *Solomonic Love and Sex Model*.

Solomonic Love and Sex Model
In the Solomonic model, he went after the Shulamite using what turned her on. He esteemed her by talking adoringly about her wonderful attributes. He complimented her loveliness and lavished her with praise concerning her ravishing beauty:

> "You are altogether beautiful,
> my darling, and there is no blemish in you"
> (Song of Solomon 4:7 NASB).

Solomon continued wooing her with affirmation. Moment by moment he adores her hair, cheekbones, lips, eyes, and belly. He expanded poetically, using symbolic prose, to lovingly describe their sexual engagement. Whatever the words, there is no question that he showered her with praise, with adoration, and with appreciation. He delighted in every aspect of her very being, personhood, and her sexuality.

In return, the Shulamite invited Solomon to come near, physically, emotionally, mentally, and spiritually.

What did Solomon's adoration do to her?

Solomon's expression of affirmation ignited her passion powerfully. She felt adored, accepted, and appreciated. She wanted him closer, so she invited him to taste the sexual "fruits" of her body.

Hear the words of the Song of Solomon to his bride:

> *Epic lovers have the right to mutual sexual fulfillment in marriage.*

The Fearless Lover

> "Awake, O north wind,
> And come, wind of the south;
> Make my garden breathe out fragrance,
> Let its spices be wafted abroad.
> May my beloved come into his garden
> And eat its choice fruits!" (4:16 NASB).

As she was adored, she invited him to taste of her fruits and drink of her wine. We assume this is meant to be both a literal and a figurative tasting. She invited him at her pace and asked for the degree of physical involvement she preferred. Solomon did not hesitate in his response to her invitation. He responded with more words of affirmation.

> "I have come into my garden,
> My sister, my bride;
> I have gathered my myrrh along with my balsam.
> I have eaten my honeycomb and my honey;
> I have drunk my wine and my milk" (5:1 NASB).

The Formula

As noted from Solomon's model, the husband and wife's love-making dynamics are expressions as follows:
  A. **A**ppreciation and affirmation, which leads to acceptance
  B. **B**enevolence—she extends a sexual invitation. His adoration of her arouses her passion.
  C. **C**onsummation—love making follows

Solomon surrendered his rights as a husband in wanting sex to focus on his bride, the Shulamite's needs!

Epic lovers have the right to mutual sexual fulfillment in marriage. There is no doubt that God designed and intended for sexual enjoyment in marriage. Sex was meant to be a vital aspect of the marriage and an ongoing expectation between partners to bring satisfaction in all areas of their lives—emotionally, physically, and spiritually.

While as a husband, you have a right to be sexually satisfied and fulfilled by your wife, you must play your part first before you seek after your own pleasure. Christ's right was to be equal with God; but, because of His love for the church, He gave up that right. Thus, you may have to give up your right for sexual pleasure and fulfillment with your wife to show your FEARLESS love to her as Christ showed His love for the church.

The apostle Paul provides more information to guide men when he says, "Do nothing out of selfish ambition or vain conceit. Rather in humility value others above yourself, not looking to your own interests, but each of you to the interests of others" (Philippians 2:3-4 NIV).

Somebody may be saying, "Dr. Vassell and Jenny, the use of that Scripture was too farfetched, and it is twisting Scripture." Not really, according to George Gilder's, *Men and Marriage*,

> It is men who make the major sacrifice. The man renounces his dream of short-term sexual freedom and self-fulfillment, his male sexuality and self-expression, to serve a woman and family for a lifetime. It is a traumatic act of giving up his most profound yearning, his longing for the hunt and the chase, the motorbike and the open road, and immediate excitement. This male sacrifice ... is essential to civilization.[5]

It sounds like a touch of what Christ did for humanity.

Your Investment Will Pay a Great Dividend.

If you are to love your wife as Christ loved the church, it means you are to regard her sexual needs as just as important as yours. You have a responsibility to seek and know her sexual needs. You can know her needs if you create an atmosphere of freedom for her to express these needs without being inhibited.

To a man of God and more so, an epic lover, sex is a joyous gift from God the Creator of all good things. It is high time that you commit yourself to enjoy it to the maximum within the sanctity of your marriage . . . just the way God ordained it. Your wife, lover, and friend is expecting you to; and guess what, she too wants to enjoy it with you! You do not want to fake your Christian experience by hiding your sexual needs. Ask for God's guidance through prayer and practice. Do not fake it; live it! Let the Holy Spirit be your guide as you minister, yes that is what we said . . . minister to your spouse. Let the love oil flow!

REVIEW QUESTIONS

1. What is ED?

2. Is ED a dysfunction of only older men?

3. What can men do to control ED?

4. What are the effects of ED when it goes untreated?

5. What is the ABC Solomonic Love and Sex Model?

END NOTES

[1] Steve Harvey, *Act Like a Lady, Think Like a Man* (New York: Amistad Publishing, a division of HarperCollins, 2009).

[2] Edward O. Laumann, it.al., *The Social Organization of Sexuality: Sex and Practices in the United States* (Chicago: University of Chicago Press, 1004).

[3] Daniel Vassell, *Love Factor in Marriage* (Lake Mary Florida: Creation House, 2005).

[4] Richard Sine, "Sex Drive: How Do Men and Women Compare?" WebMD. https://www.webmd.com/sex/features/sex-drive-how-do-men-women-compare#1.

[5] George Gilder, *Men and Marriage* (Gretna, LA: Pelican Publishing Company, 1992), p. 171.

The EPIC MARRIAGE

Chapter 8

THE DELICATE LOVER
(Designed to Be ... a Godly and Sensuous Woman)

Does body image play a major role in a woman's sexuality? Do feelings or looks have anything to do with women and their sexuality? The couples' therapy expert, Esther Perel, wisely points out that women's vision of themselves may be more crucial to desire than their relationship is to their partners. "Over and above anyone else," she writes, "Women are their own point of reference for how sexy they are."[1] This self-scrutiny plays out most obviously and agonizingly in their body image. The birds and bees and other animals do it without much thought, but not women! Women's body image matters a great deal in their sexuality! A reader may say this is very secular reasoning. So, how do you reconcile this view with the Word of God? We will get to that question later.

Women need to feel loved, appreciated, affirmed, cherished, and sensual to fully embrace the gift of love and sex that God has wired them with and for, without feelings of shame or guilt. The attitude of dishonor surrounding female sexuality needs to stop in our culture and, sad to say, even within the sacred confines of the organized church.

God created women as sexual beings; yet in most intimate relationships, Christian women often do not know how to express themselves, both as sexual and spiritual beings. The examples we (Jenny speaking) see around us teach us to objectify ourselves, rather than celebrate our sexuality as a gift from God. We often find ourselves reacting to being sexualized, rather than expressing our own God-given desires.

A poor body image does not just inhibit sexual desires in women—but it can hijack the view of their entire sexuality.

From the beginning, God created women to be the more refined and interesting of His two created human beings (Genesis 1:27; 1 Peter 3:7). God crafted women expressly to be an epitome of beauty (Jeremiah 1:5), and in ways difficult to understand. Not only is the woman's physical appearance important to God, but it was also a direct attraction to Adam—he exclaimed when he saw Eve, "This is now bone of my bones and flesh of my flesh" (Genesis 2:23). Adam recognized Eve in her beautiful image and glory!

A poor body image does not just inhibit sexual desires in women—but it can hijack the view of their entire sexuality. In a 2010 study of 154 women published in the *Journal of Sexual Medicine* by Cindy Meston, concludes that women who had low self-esteem and thought about physical appearance during sex had less satisfying sex and were more distressed about their sex lives. Simply speaking, women will enjoy their sexuality best if the candles are scented just right, if they feel good about themselves, and if their emotional connection sparks their sexual desires.[2]

In Chapter 7, we stated it clearly—husbands love sex! Now, wives, we know that you are waiting to hear a pronouncement that describes you. Well, here it goes: women love sex too! There, we said it. However, sex is a little bit more complicated for women than it is for men! Why is it complicated?

The challenge for many wives, especially some good Christian women, is that they cannot fathom the combination of the words godly and sensuous. Their definition of a godly woman does not include the words "sensuous" or "sexual." Many Christian women in their quest to become godly believe they must deny or repress their sensuality. As a result, they will either withhold or fake sexual ecstasy during sexual intimacy, while their partner is enjoying the experience.

One of God's greatest gifts to humanity is the ability to experience mutual sexual satisfaction in the sexual encounter between married couples. Many Christian women believe that God created them to be sensual, and that He fashioned their bodies to fit in perfect harmony with their husband's. However, there are many wives steeped in faulty biblical theology, and they are unable to fully appreciate and express themselves sexually because they were culturally conditioned to repress their sexuality. You may be wondering why we have difficulty harmonizing our theology with sexual practices. Simply speaking, it is because of faulty theological concepts about sex.

Many Christian counselors believe the main reasons Christian women are unable to harmonize their theology with practice is largely due to the fact they view the word "sensuous" in a negative way. If that is true, let us begin this discussion by looking at the definition of the word sensuous.

> *To be sensuous is a natural biological response to your unique bodily function.*

Webster's Dictionary defines *sensuous* as, "pertaining to the senses; appealing to the senses, alive to the pleasure to be received through the senses." Although the word sensuous is a positive term, it is often viewed negatively, to describe unhealthy and unrestrained sexual conduct (see Galatians 5:19). We submit to you that to be sensuous means, "to be alive to the pleasures received through the God-created senses."

To be sensuous is a natural biological response to your unique bodily function. If that is the definition of sensuousness, why do some Christian wives have difficulty expressing themselves in sensuous ways in their relationships? One reason some women who marry find it difficult to suddenly open up is because they spent so many years "repressing" their sexual passions to remain pure. They find it difficult to suddenly open the floodgates of their emotions and allow sexual feelings to flow. Furthermore, some women have ignored their sexuality for too long so now it has atrophied. They have a negative view of sex, thereby repressing their sexual feelings, considering it as evil and demonic. It is time to exorcise those demons, in order to have a cognitive restructuring—a restructuring that will put sex in its proper context. This will be a revolution emancipating women to appreciate the liberty and benefits of sexual and marital happiness.

Yet, another reason for difficulty in exercising sensuality is many women are unable to forgive themselves for past sexual sins. They feel that part of their self-flagellation is to never fully enjoy the benefits of sexual fulfillment.

Wives, Jenny and I believe that the culture of the world has perverted God's gift of sex, and as a result, many Christian wives feel they must shun anything associated with the erotic or sensuous, in order to appear godly. No, sisters! God wants you to be both godly and sensuous in your marital relationships. The goal of an epic lover is, to maintain a balance between being sensual, sexual, and godly. So, how does an epic lover create that balance? We will answer that question later in the chapter. Now let us address a few more general sexual inhibitors that have limited or repressed godly wives' sexual desires.

Researchers have consistently stated that there are three main reasons married women are losing their sexual desire while being married. They are: (1) a feeling of unattractiveness, (2) lack of excitement, and (3) low overall satisfaction in life.

Feeling Unattractive

We started the chapter discussing the role of body image in regard to women's sexuality. "Sisters, you know we (Jenny speaking) need more than intimacy to feel sensual, we want to feel comfortable in our bodies, especially when we are undressed. Women who are uncomfortable with themselves tend to lose interest in sex. Their sexual desire declines! On the other hand, when they feel comfortable with their bodies, coupled with a corresponding sense of sexual attractiveness, they tend to find sex more gratifying and not just another chore.

Low Overall Satisfaction From Life

Another reason women lose their sex desire is often connected to relationship issues. Sexual feelings are connected to every part of a women's being. So, wives can be very happy with their husbands, but unhappy with their daily lives. Their marriages could be overstressed, overloaded with work, and simply boring with their predictable lives. Consequently, they are unmotivated because their lives are at a standstill. This general discontent and boredom can take its toll on wives' sexual desires. It becomes even more challenging when wives have children and work outside their homes, returning to do the household chores with little or no help from their husbands. This is a big-time sex killer!

Lack of Excitement

The third and final point is, marital sex can become socially sanctioned, sanitized, predictable, and mundane and many wives find it tiresome and routine. Some wives are dopamine deprived or lacking estrogen. Dopamine is a neurotransmitter that fuels sexual desire to rise in response to anticipation and excitement. Estrogen, on the other hand, provides an essential role in the growth and development of female secondary sexual characteristics. The cure to this dilemma is for couples to take the time to initiate some creativity in their sexual approaches so as to release dopamine. The brain chemicals alone cannot fix the lack of excitement; couples need to use their creativity to jump-start the love chemicals in the brain. If it is an estrogen issue, wives need to seek professional assistance.

Sex Drives and Age

Scientists are of the persuasion that a woman's sex drive decreases with the onset of aging. Conversely, the opposite is true as observed by Dr. Maureen McGrath, RN, a sex-health educator and radio host, who says: "It is more likely for younger women to experience dips in libido, which could be caused by the hormonal disruptions of pregnancy, childbirth, breastfeeding, and dealing with young children."[3] Do not attribute your lack of sex

Epic couples understand the importance of sexual frequency, so they make creative plans to invest quality time for lovemaking.

or diminishment of the sex drive to aging, there could be other factors.

The number of times epic couples have sex per week or month has nothing to do with age, it has everything to do with choices. Epic lovers are never too busy to have time for sex, because they realize it is an important part of their lives. Epic couples understand the importance of sexual frequency, so they make creative plans to invest quality time for lovemaking.

What Are Some Causes of Low Sex Drive?

If wives care for themselves holistically, that is, physically, mentally, emotionally, psychologically, spiritually, and relationally, they should possess a robust and healthy sex drive

... unless they are suffering from one of the itemized issues listed below:

- Physical issues, including hormonal changes related to menopause, childbirth, or thyroid problems.
- Chronic stress, included in your relationship.
- Depression or other mental health issues.
- Some prescription drugs may also affect libido, including some types of antidepressants, birth control pills, anti-anxiety drugs, and blood pressure medications.

Leah Millheiser, MD, director of the Female Sexual Medicine Program at Stanford University School of Medicine, says: "If you have pain during sex, for instance, over time you may develop low sexual desire."[4] Sisters, do not diagnose yourself. If you are experiencing any of the above issues, and you and your husband have prayed, and there is no change, please go see your medical practitioner and discuss it.

Reviving Your Libido

Many couples tend to self-diagnose and treat their problems to avoid exposing their condition! Epic couples always choose to be open and seek for the best ways to address their marital issues. Generally, ordinary married couples tend to feel embarrassed and ashamed. Libido problems are very common. Do not live a mediocre sex life when there are options available to you. To secure the most appropriate care and results for your libido problem, consult your medical doctor or a counselor to address these concerns.

> *Godly wives need to know that spiritual intimacy and delights are not in opposition to sensual feelings and delights.*

If your doctor seems uncomfortable or unconcerned when you bring up your sexual problems, do not give up; ask for a referral to see a gynecologist or a sex therapist who will assist you in dealing with your sexual dysfunction. It is God's desire for you to be whole and well.

Be Who You Were Created to Be

Jenny and I have had a wonderful time researching and writing about the medical and psychosocial issues regarding sex drives, because we feel it is necessary to the health and well-being of all epic married couples. We believe that marital sex involves a greater level of knowledge, and we want to minimize all distractions so couples, especially wives, can experience the quality sexual fulfillment in their marriages.

Godly wives need to know that spiritual intimacy and delights are not in opposition to sensual feelings and delights. To validate this view, doctors Dan Allender and Tremper Longman, in their book, *Intimate Allies*, say: "A taste of the character of God is found in sexual foreplay, heightened arousal, and orgasm. God is a God of passion. He adores joy, and He delights in our delight.[5]

Women, your sensuality, sexuality, and spirituality are not separate and divided as many would want you to believe. Rather, they form a circle—a whole and unbroken being. Linda Dillow and Lorraine Pintus, in their book, *Intimate Issues: Twenty-one Questions Christians Ask About Sex*, quoted Vignette Bright's beautiful description of the circle of women's sensuality, spirituality, and sexuality, when she says,

> It is as important to be filled with the Spirit in bed with your husband, ministering to him (as he ministers to you as well) as it is for you to be filled with the Spirit when you are teaching the Bible or ministering.[6]

Perhaps the most powerful illustration of the union between our sensuality and spirituality is revealed in the Song of Solomon.

Dillow and Pintus continue to expand this by saying, "In this beautiful love story, we find Solomon the "Lover," and Shulamite, the "Beloved," engaged in a steamy, erotic, sensuous lovemaking without losing godliness. Suddenly, a third Person—God—appears in the room. Tenderly, the Almighty Creator gazes upon the lovers engaged in physical pleasures and extends His hand in spiritual blessing: "Eat, friends; drink and imbibe deeply, O lovers" (Song of Solomon 5:1 NASB).

Dillow and Pintus encouraged their readers to visualize that God is present. He sees your true passion. He hears the sighs of delight. He watches the lovers as they caress one another in the most intimate ways and places. He is witness to the fleshly, earthy sights, touch, sounds, and smells. He sees it all, and then He urges the lovers to feast and drink abundantly of the beautiful pleasures He created for both to relish.

It is God's desire for all women to rejoice in their natural response of their sensuousness within marriage. God wants you as a wife to open the floodgates of your physical passion and immerse yourself in it. "Drink and imbibe deeply," He urges. It is therefore important for couples to know that while enjoying and displaying their sensuality, they are yielding to the Holy Spirit's leading and guidance.

Being a Sensuous and Sexual Woman for My Husband and Me!

The Shulamite in the Song of Solomon is a model of a sensuous wife. What made her such an exceptional wife that she moved the heart of her lover to write about their marriage? She must have done something to outshine all the other wives and concubines. What could that be?

The story is narrated in poetic language to inspire, inform, and to be a model for couples. And as such, we believe the Bible would not be complete without this story. This story should let all couples know that if God was excited about Solomon and the Shulamite experience, He is equally happy about His children today.

Now, let us unpack the Shulamite woman's story and see a little more of what a loving, godly, and sensuous woman she was, shining in all her feminine glory. According to Dillow and Pintus:

If the Shulamite woman could dance and make herself pleasing for her husband, you can too.

The Delicate Lover

First, she was receptive. She whispered longingly into Solomon's ear, "Make my garden breathe out fragrance, let its spices be wafted abroad. May my beloved come into his garden and eat its choice fruits" (Song of Solomon 4:16 NASB). The Shulamite is opening up to her man and getting ready to enjoy him. She was showing her emotion, heart, mind, and body to Solomon as she invites him into her garden without restrictions. She removes all walls.

Second, she is courageous and uninhibited. She passionately goes after her lover. She was not afraid to be the initiator, by aggressively stimulating her lover with intoxicating fragrances, seductive sights, and the promise of sexual pleasure. There in the garden laden with sweet smelling fruits and vines, she offered him old and new sexual delights (see Song of Solomon 7:11-13).

Third, the Shulamite woman is candid and real (see Song of Solomon 2:6; 4:16). She tantalizes him with an erotic dance as an invitation to lovemaking (7:1-3). She did not hold back her feelings and body. She realized that God made her husband to be stimulated by what he sees. She used the sense of looking, feeling, smelling, and touching... do I need to say more? She was using all the senses.[7]

I know some readers may be thinking that since Jenny and I are Christians, this kind of talk is too risqué. In other words, sex is something you do, but don't talk about. Well, if this disclosure offends your sensitivities, may I remind you that this is indelibly written in the sacred book? Yes, we are reading from the Bible. If the Shulamite woman could dance and make herself pleasing for her husband, you can too.

Listen to me, women of God, it is time to remove the barriers that have been keeping you from fully enjoying and experiencing sexual fulfillment in your marriage. Breaking through these traditional barriers may require the Holy Spirit's guidance and counseling. The Holy Spirit is waiting on you to call on Him, and I know when you call and yield yourself to Him, He will remove your walls of fear, intimidation, or whatever it is that has been holding you back. I know some of you just want to stop right here and go get your husband, but if you read on, you may learn some more from the Shulamite woman

> *If the Shulamite woman could dance and make herself pleasing for her husband, you can too.*

Fourth, the Shulamite was doing what most women love best, communication. She does not leave Solomon to read her mind, she verbalizes her thoughts: "My beloved is mine and I am his" (Song of Solomon 2:16 NASB). She expresses praise for her husband's masculinity: "How handsome you are, my beloved" (1:16). "Like an apple tree among the trees of the forest, so is my beloved among the young men" (2:3). She is not afraid to praise her man for his masculinity. She takes time to affirm the significance of her man! These words would gain the full attention of any man. Why? One of the greatest masculine needs is the need for significance!

The Delicate Lover

Last, the Shulamite woman is sensuous. As a sensuous woman, she is in tune with her body and the stimulation she receives through her five senses. She delights in her senses. In Song of Solomon 5:10-16, the Shulamite woman gives in to her sexual feelings while thinking about her husband in very sensuous terms."[8]

Please note: Although Solomon was absent, the Shulamite meditates on her husband's body, describing him with erotic imagery. In her mind, she was undressing Solomon, beginning at the top of his head and working her way downward. She dwells on his sensuous lips, his muscular shoulders, his strong legs, and then ends her daydreaming by saying: "His mouth is full of sweetness. And he is wholly desirable" (5:16). The Shulamite's thoughts prepared her to act out her sensuousness with her husband.

No doubt about it, the Shulamite was a sensuous, sexual woman—and God allowed Solomon to describe her sensuousness in explicit and erotic terms. God wants us to understand the beauty and freedom of our sexuality. Through the Shulamite woman's narrative, God unveils a model of a loving, godly, sensuous wife, and because His blessing is upon her, we can follow her example with confidence.

If you are thinking, I could never be like that, do not be discouraged. God does not expect us to become sensuous saints overnight. Instead, He asks that we go forward today, little by little in becoming the lovers He created us to be. Christian women should be the greatest lovers on earth because, as believers, we not only possess physical passion, but also we can infuse holiness into our sensuousness.

The Gracefulness of a Sensuous Woman

Daniel and I know that the way you view your body image plays a major role in being sensuous. Women tend to find it difficult to use their body to please their husbands, if they are feeling unattractive or not sexy. What does it mean to be attractive? Webster defines *attractive* as, "having the quality of attracting; having the power to charm; being alluring, inviting, engaging, enticing." But it is difficult to feel attractive when in your thoughts, you feel you are not!

> *It is better to be sensuous than to have a perfect petite size "4" body.*

Let us look at the second word, sexy. According to Andrew Greeley, author of *Sexual Intimacy*, to be *sexy* is "to be aware of your body as an instrument of playfulness and delight, to be able to communicate this awareness to your husband and give him the gift of your body for pleasure, delight, variety, and playfulness."[9]

Women! It is better to be sensuous than to have a perfect petite size "4" body. Your husbands will find more delight in your being gentle and sensuous than in your being a figure 4! Listen to scriptures that speak about the kind of woman you can be to keep your husband excited: Delighting your husband with your breasts and giving him ecstasy (see Proverbs 5:19), and dancing, revealing the beauty of your body before him (see Song of Solomon 6:13–7:9) will cause him to celebrate the joy of your body. Your body in its beauty is God's gift to your husband. Your body is for him just as his body is for you! My husband's body and my body are far from perfect, and they will continue to age. But I am committed to continue learning to be an expert at using my body to intoxicate my husband, Daniel, with passion and excitement, and you should do likewise for your husband.

What Do Men Look At?

For many wives who seek to be both attractive and sexy, the major question that needs to be answered is what do men look for in a woman or what do they see first when they see one? So, what do you think men look at first when they see a woman? If you answer, "her body," you are wrong. According Dillow and Pintus in *Intimate Issues*, a *USA Today* survey, 39 percent of men say the first things they notice are eyes. Next highest (25 percent) is the smile or teeth. Only 14 percent say the first thing they notice is the body.[10] Another survey says, **Your Eyes.** Seventy percent of men say they notice a woman's eyes first. Our eyes tell us a great deal about our personality.

So, the body is important. Next question is what kind of body do you think attracts men? Do you think men prefer the supermodel look? No. The average man finds normal-weighted women sexier than very thin women. This was the conclusion of Dr. Devendra Singh, University of Texas psychologist, after showing pictures of twelve female shapes to seven hundred men. We try to laugh off our new roll of fat or our size double A breasts with comments like, "I'm so flat you could land airplanes on my chest" or "My legs look like tree stumps." But such degrading comments can sabotage our body image and cause us to feel unattractive when we are naked in the bedroom. We would feel more attractive if our bodies looked a certain way— if we had a perfect "10" body. But Dr. John Gray, author of the famed *Men Are from Mars, Women Are from Venus* says, "When a man is in love and turned on by his wife, he is also totally entranced by the feminine beauty of her body, regardless of where the media would rank it on a scale of one to ten. When he is in love with his wife, he experiences the perfection of her body for him."[11]

The issue for you personally is what is attractive to your husband? Most men prefer women who are average weight, but some men like women who are overweight. Others like the hard body type. Some men like women with the glamour image and lots of makeup. Others prefer the natural look. Rather than seeking to please fashion critics, we should seek to please the man God gave us to love. Your husband was attracted to your body and all your other physical features. You allured and captivated him with your smile, eyes, body, intelligence, and personality.

Be the woman God has created you to be. Be godly, sensuous, sexy, and smart.

He chose you among all the women in the world. It was not just your body he liked, it was you. It does not matter if you are 4 feet, 11 inches and have a short waist, or 5 feet, 11 inches and have long legs. If you do the most with what you have, your body will please and excite your husband.

Women, I urge you to be proud of your sexuality and sensuality. First, let us use our bodies to shine for God who made it in His own image and likeness. Use them to bring glory to God. Do not be confused with how the mind is thinking; believe what God's Word says about you.

Women, be yourself! Be the woman God has created you to be. Be godly, sensuous, sexy, and smart. Allow the Holy Spirit to guide you as you enjoy this new relationship and begin to increase your health benefits from having sex. We will close this chapter with an article written by Kathleen Doheny featured on *WebMD* titled, "10 Surprising Health Benefits of Sex."

1. *Less Stress, Better Blood Pressure*: Having sex could lower your stress and blood pressure. That finding

comes from a Scottish study of 24 women and 22 men who kept records of their sexual activity. The researchers put them in stressful situations—such as speaking in public and doing math out loud—and checked their blood pressure. People who had had sex responded better to stress than those who engaged in other sexual behaviors or abstained.

2. *Sex Boosts Immunity*: Having sex once or twice a week has been linked with higher levels of an antibody called immunoglobulin A, or IgA, which can protect you from getting colds and other infections. A Wilkes University study had 112 college students keep records of how often they had sex and provide saliva samples for the study. Those who had sex once or twice a week had higher levels of IgA than other students.

3. *Sex Burns Calories*: Thirty minutes of sex burns 85 calories or more. "Sex is a great mode of exercise," Los Angeles sexologist Patti Britton says. "It takes both physical and psychological work to do it well," she says.

4. *Sex Improves Heart Health*: A 20-year-long British study shows that men who had sex two or more times a week were half as likely to have a fatal heart attack than men who had sex less than once a month. And although some older folks may worry that sex could cause a stroke, the study found no link between how often men had sex and how likely they were to have a stroke. This will benefit your husband more, and it will keep him alive and around for a longer time with you.

5. *Better Self-Esteem*: University of Texas researchers found that boosting self-esteem was one of 237 reasons people have sex. "Great sex begins with

self-esteem. If the sex is loving, connected, and what you want, it raises it." Of course, you do not have to have lots of sex to feel good about yourself. Your self-esteem is all about you, not someone else. But if you are already feeling good about yourself, a great sex life may help you feel even better.

6. *Deeper Intimacy*: Having sex and orgasms boosts levels of the hormone oxytocin, the so-called love hormone, which helps people bond and build trust. In a study of 59 women, researchers checked their oxytocin levels before and after the women hugged their partners. The women had higher oxytocin levels if they had more of that physical contact with their partner. Higher oxytocin levels have also been linked with a feeling of generosity. So, snuggle up—it might help you feel more generous toward your partner.

7. *Sex May Turn Down Pain*: Oxytocin also boosts your body's painkillers, called endorphins. Headache, arthritis pain, or PMS symptoms may improve after sex. In one study, 48 people inhaled oxytocin vapor and then had their fingers pricked. The oxytocin increased their pain threshold by more than half, meaning they sensed pain at a higher threshold or were more tolerant of pain.

8. *More Ejaculations May Make Prostate Cancer Less Likely*: Research shows that frequent ejaculations, especially in 20-something men, may lower the risk of getting prostate cancer later in life. A study published in the *Journal of the American Medical Association* found that men who had 21 or more ejaculations a month were less likely to get prostate cancer than those who had four to seven ejaculations per month.

9. *Stronger Pelvic Floor Muscles*: For women, doing pelvic floor muscle exercises called Kegels may mean more pleasure—and, as a perk, less chance of incontinence later in life. Finally!
10. *Better Sleep*: The oxytocin released during orgasm also helps sleep, research shows. Getting enough sleep has also been linked with a host of other health benefits, such as a healthy weight and better blood pressure. That is something to think about, especially if you have been wondering why your guy can be active one minute and snoring the next.[12]

REVIEW QUESTIONS

1. How did Webster's dictionary define *sensuous*?

2. What are the three main reasons given for women's lack of or low sexual desires?

3. Discuss the importance of estrogen and dopamine in relationship to a woman's sex drive?

4. What can women learn from the Shulamite to improve their marriage?

5. Discuss how important body image is to women's sexuality?

END NOTES

[1] Jill Denton, LMFT, CSAT, CSE, CCS, Sexuality/Sex Therapy, in her article titled, "Women Wanting More: The Delicate Balance of Love and Desire," quoted Esther Perel, March 20, 2013. She writes, "Women are their own point of reference for how sexy they are." This self-scrutiny plays out most obviously and agonizingly in our body image. A poor body image doesn't just inhibit desire—it can hijack our view of our entire sex life. In a 2010 study of 154 women published in the Journal of Sexual Medicine, Cindy Meston concludes that women who had low self-esteem and thought about physical appearance during sex had less satisfying sex and were more distressed about their sex lives.

[2] Cindy Meston, *Journal of Sexual Medicine*, 2010.

[3] Maureen McGrath, R.N., Radio host.

[4] Jen Uscher, writing for WebMD, wrote an article "Is there a Pill for Women's Sex Drive?" This article will help women better understand their libido issues. https://www.webmd.com/women/features/is-there-a-pill-for-womens-libido#1

[5] Jenny and I recommend a book by Drs. Allender and Longman called, *Intimate Allies* (Carol Stream, Ill.: Tyndale House Publishers, Inc., 1999). We consider it a must read for epic lovers who would like to maximize their intimacy.

[6] Another good book is written by Linda Dillow and Lorraine Pintus titled, *Intimate Issues* (Colorado Springs, CO: Waterbrook Press, 1999). This is a must read.

[7] Dillon and Pintres, Ibid.

[8] Ibid.

[9] Andrew Greeley, *Sexual Intimacy: Love and Play* (New York: Grand Central Publishing, 1988).

[10] *Intimate Issues* (page 58).

[11] John Gray, *Men Are From Mars, Woman Are From Venus* (New York: HarperCollins, 1992).

[12] http://www.cbsnews.com/news/10-surprising-health-benefits-of-sex/

The EPIC MARRIAGE

CHAPTER 9

RAVISHING LOVERS

"Rejoice with the wife of thy youth.
Let her be as the loving hind and pleasant roe;
let her breasts satisfy thee at all times;
and be thou ravished always with her love"
(Proverbs 5:18-19 KJV).

Do you remember when ravishing, loving thoughts of your beloved captured and arrested your thoughts and imagination with increasing frequency, taking you on an epic, endless journey of romance and passion? Can you remember the thrill and excitement welling up inside you in anticipation of seeing your spouse? Do you recall making fancy dinner reservations and dancing the night away, or buying big bunches of flowers and sentimental greeting cards for her? Remember when you just could not keep your hands off your other half? Maybe that seems like a very long time ago and those days appear to be far behind you since you have been together awhile. These feelings and memories never disappear for the epic lovers. These days continue in various forms and mature with time and experience.

One of the biggest challenges in most marriages today is keeping romantic and love flames burning. According to

Dr. Sheri Myers, author of *Rebuild Love* (also a marriage and family therapist and television talk show host), "When we first fall in love, the romantic thrill happens effortlessly because of pleasure-boosting hormones that create a neurochemical cocktail that drive us toward greater intimacy."[1] There is nothing quite as exhilarating as the feelings associated with the early stages of romantic love.

Medical science tells us when couples are in love, specific areas of their brains are stimulated and literally ignited! Falling in love produces a biological state that is a high like being on cocaine—the recreational drug. Research evidence has proven that you feel relaxed, and the feel-good hormone serotonin lowers, causing you to obsess about your new-found love and consistently reflect on the romantic times spent with him or her.

> *The importance of keeping the romance in your marriage in order to facilitate a robust and thriving relationship cannot be overstated.*

However, these euphoric feelings rarely last and are difficult to maintain alongside the demands and responsibilities of everyday life. Learning how to maintain the balance between romance and intimacy combined with the demands of everyday life is the greatest challenge most couples encounter in long-term relationships. Daily distractions such as work-related stress, parenting, and financial pressures, including paying bills can take its toll on relationships and conspire to gradually extinguish the romantic flame with the passage of time. Dealing with these multiple challenges has the capacity to absorb a great deal of time, energy, and focus, diverting our attention and robbing us of relational intimacy with our lover.

The importance of keeping the romance in your marriage in order to facilitate a robust and thriving relationship cannot be overstated. Dr. Myers contends that romance is "the language of love. It's the little things that we do or say that mean a lot." So, how can you and your spouse continue to sustain romance throughout marriage? The answer from an empowered, Spirit-led, living perspective is to be grounded in the Word of God. The greatest ingredient in the achievement of success is God. Remember the four pillars to a successful marriage which were previously referenced and discussed. They are: prayer; empowered, Spirit-led living; love; and service. These principles must be applied daily as you seek the Lord in prayer, while asking for wisdom and guidance from the Spirit to become the best spouse you can be to your life partner.

Christian couples do not need to lose romance in their marriage or lose the love of their lives. They need to find, create, and cultivate ways to

> **SCENARIO: Sleep Will Be Sweet**
>
> A couple has been married for six years and had their second child last year. The wife has been a stay-at-home mother to their two children. However, the husband's company recently went through a process of downsizing, and he was required to accept a decrease in salary to keep his current position. The couple decided that it was time for the wife to start working again. Within two months, she found a job. Unfortunately, things have changed dramatically, and the transition back to the workforce has been challenging. At the end of a busy work day, both the husband and wife are extremely exhausted and are only interested in one thing ... getting straight to bed to obtain as much sleep as they can.

keep their romantic love alive, which is neither impossible nor a Herculean task. God cares about you, your romantic and sexual life, as well as your spouse. Now, let us look at the Word of God and see how it helps to keep the romantic candle aflame and bright.

For many couples, maintaining the romance in marriage is an area that requires ongoing mutual effort. The example provided in the Sleep Will Be Sweet scenario is a common situation that occurs in marriage. The couple becomes preoccupied with their daily obligations to support the family and provide for their children; hence, their own needs become secondary.

The topic of romance and intimacy is very sensitive and can give rise to a great deal of secrecy coupled with negativity. This causes many couples to avoid or resist openly discussing their issues or sharing their stories. Oftentimes, the inability to self-disclose in this arena is related to the fear of being hurt or rejected by one's spouse. However uncomfortable these issues are, epic lovers find creative ways to communicate directly and lovingly about their needs, to avoid or prevent future conflicts.

To keep romance and intimacy alive, and to minimize marital infidelity, Solomon gave one of the best instructions any father could give a son. That instruction is a mantra that keeps an epic marriage couple's romance and intimacy vibrant and striving.

> ... Rejoice in the wife of your youth... .
> Let her breasts satisfy you at all times;
> be exhilarated always with her love
> (Proverbs 5:18-19 NASB).

Many scholars are of the persuasion that this is a command primarily about marital fidelity. It is a fatherly instruction by

Solomon to his son, about marital fidelity. He is instructed to enjoy his marriage and refrain from any involvement with prostitutes or other immoral women. It is a message to married couples also!

For those married couples who take time to read the Song of Solomon, note how he describes in glowing poetic language the physical bodies of the epic married lovers. Throughout this short writing, the feelings, attitudes, imaginations, dreams, spiritual joys, and the romantic happiness of these epic married lovers are beautifully portrayed.

This text was given to maintain faithfulness in his marriage. It challenged wives to keep and make themselves attractive for their husbands. It called upon husbands to utilize the power of their eyes to enchantingly capture their imagination and lead them into a romantic sphere of pleasure and intimacy with their wives. This Proverb commands marital fidelity, which if observed and maintained, will in the end discourage or prevent any semblance of infidelity.

> *Only as romance, intimacy, and sex are protected in marriage can it truly be enjoyed as God intended.*

One of the biggest problems in Christendom is that we are fully aware of what we are to avoid. We are experts of the forbidden knowledge, but naïve at the permitted knowledge.

We cannot read these words without being convinced that what Solomon has in view is romantic and sexual love in marriage. However, these delightful, loving, intimate, sexual experiences are to be placed and experienced strictly within the confines of heterosexual marriage. God has placed restraints and prohibitions in marriage to ensure that a wonderful pleasure is guaranteed and increased, while safeguarding and preserving its sanctity. Only as romance, intimacy, and sex are protected in marriage can it truly be enjoyed as God intended. The beauty with epic couples is, they allow themselves to be engaged in all the fullness of the pleasures available in marital intimacy—they choose to keep it youthful.

"Rejoice with the wife of thy youth."
Solomon instructs his son to fully embrace and enjoy marital intimacy with the wife of his youth. He wanted him to know the pleasures available in a passionate intimacy which could render one a slave of love—conquered by and surrendered to the love of one's wife. The text also reveals an interesting caveat—if you go astray, you could compromise your integrity by being conquered and enslaved by an immoral woman. Hence the warning, "Remain faithful to the wife of your youth!"

True, God-honoring pleasure protects couples against the temptations of counterfeit pleasures. Thus, the father continues to implore his son, furnishing him with fatherly wisdom in the form of descriptive poetry to love and rejoice in the wife of his youth.

With minimal knowledge and experience, a wife, it is believed, has an amazing capacity for sexual pleasure—as much as any man can handle; which means one's wife is more than any husband can handle, if he can love her properly.

Otherwise, push the right buttons! Although the woman/wife was created for the man (Genesis 2:18; I Corinthians 11:9), his greatest pleasure comes through emphasizing her pleasure (Song of Solomon 2:6-7; 8:3-4). An epic lover will always help his wife to become the best that she can be, by rejoicing in her love without due regard for the women outside his home.

"Let her be as the loving hind and pleasant roe"

The wording of this proverb is very difficult for the Western contemporary readers to understand. To understand this text, we need to read it through Hebraic literary understanding.

A *hind* is a female deer, usually of the red deer, and a *roe* is a small species of deer native to Europe and Asia. Putting these words together, would describe a small, delicate, graceful, and tender female deer. These deer were caught, tamed, and enjoyed as pets by kings and others in Solomon's time. Their refined, gentle natures were the delight of both men and women.

Coupled with Solomon's adjectives of loving and pleasant, an epic lover also sees a wonderful word picture of a delightful and prized woman worthy of love and protection.

From the commentary on the *hind* and *roe*, one will conclude that epic lovers will always view their wives this way and treat them accordingly. An epic husband should carefully treat his wife with gentle affection and patient tenderness, just as if he were caring for a loving and pleasant female deer. Paul confirmed this rule in the New Testament where he commanded men to cherish their wives—treat them with special care (Ephesians 5:28-29).

On the other hand, the epic lover's wife will do all she can to make it easy for her husband to love her. She will choose to be a delicate and gracious person deserving affection, like a loving hind and pleasant roe. She will choose her diet and exercise to maintain the resemblance of a woman's hourglass body. Yes, we said so! She will use her body boldly and unashamedly to jointly engage in and experience sexual pleasure with her husband on a regular basis. She would lavish affection, devotion, lovemaking, and praise upon him. She would honor him with her beauty and gentleness, so he would always want to have her in his company.

Breasts

Did we use the word "breasts" as a subtopic? Yes, we did. It is written in the Bible, and the lover Solomon used it. He admonished his son, "*let **her breasts satisfy** thee*" (Proverbs 5:19 KJV). God formed Eve's breasts and all other details of her body that were so marvelously appealing to Adam's eyes. When he saw her, he exclaimed, "bone of my bones and flesh of my flesh." Today, nothing has changed—men continue to be amazed, enamored, and sometimes seduced at the wonder and beauty of the feminine form. God made men to be attracted by a woman's body, and within marriage; this wonder keeps him coming back with words of praise time and time again.

It is important to know that while breasts are mentioned by name in this proverb, they are a *synecdoche** for her whole body. The Hebrew word *dadeyah*, "her breasts," occurs only here and in Ezekiel 23:3, 8, 21, and is equivalent to *dodeyah*, "*her* love." The writer was telling his son, that his wife's whole body and lovemaking should be a constant source of delight, and a wise wife will know and exploit this for their joint happiness and pleasure.

> *Every husband must choose to focus on what he has, rather than lament his fate for what he does not have. It is a command.*

---

*Synecdoche means "a part representing the whole."

This is expressed very forcibly in the Vulgate rendering, "Let her breasts inebriate thee (*indebrient te*)," which represents the strong influence that the wife's attractions are to maintain. This requires that one's wife be obligated to keep herself attractive for her own husband. Why should she keep herself attractive? Because, the eyes of her husband want to look at her in her full glory. Here, the teacher Solomon is describing enchantment which the husband is to allow the wife to exercise over him.

The perpetual importance of breasts for attraction and lovemaking is forcefully brought to our attention by Solomon's plain language. Nothing has changed; breasts are still beautiful and important in the appearance and performance of a woman (Song of Solomon 4:5; 7:1-10; Ezekiel 16:7; 23:3, 8; Hosea 2:2). Women in Solomon's day were just as concerned about their breasts as women are today (Song of Solomon 1:13; 8:8-10).

Solomon's proverb binds every husband to be joyful, happy, comfortable, and satisfied with his wife's breasts, the rest of her body, and her lovemaking. It is a choice a husband needs to make. A word of advice is needed now!

Every husband must choose to focus on what he has, rather than lament his fate for what he does not have. It is a command. The proverb here is not a suggestion, and every man can do it, if he will obey the Lord. Her body will change for various reasons, some under her control and others beyond her control. Of course, if his wife is depriving him of sexual pleasure or has let her appearance decline, it is his duty and right to correct the situation by wise and loving management of the marriage.

Husband, you have just read marital advice worth a fortune from the wisest man who ever lived, and from one who had 1,000 wives and concubines (I Kings 11:3). Marital happiness, fulfilling love, satisfying romance, intimacy, and sex are dependent on you. The advice is simple: consider and treat her delicately with tender affection, choose to be always satisfied with her body and lovemaking, and focus on her devotion, love, and loyalty. This will bring you immense happiness and joy!

Do not allow another woman to compete with your wife's place in the marriage. Solomon's words are very valuable for promoting a great marriage, but they were given to ward off the temptations of the strange woman. By exalting your wife to her rightful place, you will

be protected from the inconvenient draw of other women who seek to tease, exasperate, and ultimately destroy you. There is no true peace, pleasure, or prosperity for an adulterer, whether the adultery is emotional, virtual, or physical. The Word of God is simple—just do not look, text, or think about another woman (Proverbs 6:25; Job 31:1; Matthew 5:28).

Contentment Is Crucial to an Enraptured Marriage.

Solomon instructed his son in the text, but we want to include daughter as well to make three important choices that will lead him/her to contentment:

1. Cherish each other tenderly as a delicate object of affection.
2. Appreciate his/her body and sexuality.
3. Let affection and devotion consume him/her.

Even though the text was written by Solomon, the teacher, to his son and student, the lesson is applicable to females as well. The metaphor of the hind and doe is not transferable to the male gender, because the text references a son. In that time and culture, boys were the only ones allowed to go to school. Also, the culture of that time was patriotic. Today's education is opened to all sexes and the issue of fidelity in marriage is equally the responsibility of both sexes. However, continuing from the original Hebrew thinking, the text is so strongly worded that in grasping for suitable words, a renowned Bible scholar decided that even the expression "love-ecstasy" was not intense enough.[2]

"Be exhilarated always with her love."

The usage of this word rendered "exhilarated" usually means either to be intoxicated, or to go astray, to be deceived. The connection between these varied meanings is that standard, rational behavior has been overridden. Something has so overwhelmed a person that cautious, controlled thinking has gone out the window. The love chemical has overtaken reason in a safe setting.

These words are saying, "within the sacredness of marriage, intentionally deepen your passions until you can hardly think straight; habitually so inflame your feelings for your partner that you lose control." Husbands are instructed to bring themselves to the point where they are driven by desire for their wives; to so incite their passions that they are repetitively captivated by their wives' sensual appeals. Consider these various translations of Proverbs 5:19:

> "Go overboard; get as high as you possibly can, as often as you can. Repeatedly, stir up your passions so that you will find your wife's delights overpoweringly seductive."

The NIV says it. "Ever be captivated by her love" (NIV 1984).

The Amplified Bible puts it, "Always be transported with delight..." and it renders the very same word in the next verse "be infatuated" (AMPC).

"Let her breasts satisfy you at all times" (NKJV).

The word interpreted "satisfy" usually means to be soaked or to drink one's fill; to have one's desire fully satisfied. The teacher seems to be saying, *drink your fill of your wife's marital pleasure; continually find total satisfaction in her.*

James Moffatt translated the last two lines:

> "Let her breasts give you rapture,
> let her love ever ravish you.[3]

God's Word urges each husband to make a continual effort to get intoxicated on his wife's love. It goes way beyond saying, "Avoid committing adultery." It essentially tells husbands: "Go overboard; get as high as you possibly can, as often as you can. Repeatedly, stir up your passions so that you will find your wife's delights overpoweringly seductive." No other woman can compete! In another way, Solomon says, do not merely let nature take its course; get so focused on her, so entranced by her that she floods your brain with love chemicals.

Someone may be saying that this is impossible. Remember who was giving the instruction. It was given by Solomon, a man whom Scripture says had unique wisdom. Solomon received divine insight and was supernaturally guided to express the specific truth God wants humanity to grasp. Is it possible? Yes! Solomon is giving his son and us, the readers, the revelation of God, Creator of sex and the very One who designed and made you and me, and He knows every cell in our bodies and every thought that has ever passed through our heads. God could not have chosen a more qualified person to share this new insight than a man who had more than 1,000 wives. He must have had a great deal to share.

Ravishing Lovers

Many scholars omitted the words, "at all times," but it was penned in the Hebrew writing.

> "Let her breasts give you rapture *at all times*, let her love ever [*or always*] ravish you."

As originally penned, the verse highlights the fact that this obsession with one's spouse should be a continual exercise. This truth applies whether one's wife is absent or present. Job (from the oldest book in the Bible) determined in his heart that he would never look cravingly (lustfully) at any woman other than his wife.

> I made a covenant with my eyes not to look lustfully at a girl . . . If my heart has been enticed by a woman, or if I have lurked at my neighbor's door, then may my wife grind another man's grain, and may other men sleep with her. For that would have been shameful, a sin to be judged. It is a fire that burns to destruction (Job 31:1, 9-12 NIV 1984).

To keep Job's vow, as well as an epic lover's vow, this attitude had to dominate one's behavior, not only when his wife was near, but also whenever any woman was in sight. Epic lovers are not merely interested in avoiding promiscuity; they want to do everything that lies in their power to delight in their partner. God refers to Ezekiel's wife as being the delight of his eyes (see Ezekiel 24:16). God's way to fight temptation is not merely by avoiding the negative, but, wherever applicable, by accentuating the positive.

Someone once said,

> "Sexuality and romantic attraction are each a wild stallion that can be tamed to become

> a faithful friend. Let it run wild and you are in grave danger of a tragic fall. Abuse it and it might even trample you to death. Treat it wisely, however, and it will serve you well. Harness its power, and it will take you to wonders that others only dream about."

Our loving Father is the author of pleasure; He will ensure that the quality and sanctity of the epic lovers' sexuality and romance never be violated, because His Spirit resides and guides His children in every sphere of life.

Hollywood, Playboy, Bollywood, and Nollywood do not set the standard for epic lovers' pleasure. Television, Internet, videos, DVDs, and magazines are not where epic lovers gain ideas and insight for marital pleasure. The Word of God and the Spirit's guidance are enough to release the tiger and keep it under control.

"Let her love ever [*or always*] ravish you."

The dictionary defines the word *ravish* as the following: "To subject to a magical influence; bewitch, or to delight to a high degree." When readers look at the word *ravish*, generally what comes to mind is, to seize and carry it away by violent force, as plundering spoil from an enemy. Another view is to ravish a person, to overpower them and take them away, as in sweeping them off their feet! This is not the message here. The message here is that epic lovers choose to be overcome by their wives' affection, devotion, lovemaking, and her wholeness. The instruction here is not ravishing your wife, but rather being ravished by your wife. It is a choice to be spoiled by her and her affection, so that a strange woman has no means of approach or seduction.

> *Being a ravishing lover begins on the inside.*

Ravishing Lovers

Being a ravishing lover begins on the inside. It starts with your appreciation for your wife. You are totally focused on her. You are open to her and to the divine.

The word translated "ravished" in this verse is *shahgah*, which means to err, go astray. It occurs about 20 times in the Old Testament, and always, except in this verse, describes *negative behavior*. That is true even in the immediate context, where Solomon uses it in verse 23 ("go astray"), as if to make sure we know he is using a negative word.

It seems Solomon is instructing his son to "go astray," to err! However, God never commands us to sin, but this almost sounds like it. It is contrasted with verse 20, where the command is to *not* "err" (same word however one translates it) with an immoral woman. Modern translations have used words such as "intoxicated," "captivated," "exhilarated," "infatuated," and "be lost."

The unique use of the negative Hebrew word *shahgah* in a positive context, near its negative use (verse 23), shows Solomon wants his readers to notice he is doing something unusual with words.

If he wanted to simply convey intoxication, as the most popular modern translations render it, the normal word would be *shawkar*. This is Hebrew poetry, using vivid language and word pictures, but why did Solomon use this particular word in this way?

The AV translators found an answer in another Hebrew word which is very close in form, *shahgal*. It occurs in four Scriptures and is twice translated "ravished" (Isaiah 13:16 and Zechariah 14:2, the others are Deuteronomy 28:30 and Jeremiah 3:2). In at least three of the four, it describes women being enslaved and physically humiliated by a conquering army.

It appears that the use of *shah-gah*, so close to *shah-gal*, in a passage using very direct language to describe physical intimacy in marriage, is intentional. This is poetic language with unusual wording to give one meaning while also bringing another word to mind—a pun, a play on words. The point of poetic or picturesque wording is to cause a reader to reflect, and in this case, the author wants his readers to reflect on both meanings. Solomon used *shahgah* in a way never used elsewhere, to bring *shahgal* to the mind of a Hebrew reader and thus convey these God-ordained purposes for pleasure in marital intimacy.

According to Bible scholars, the Hebrew word *shahgah* is never translated "be ravished" elsewhere in Scripture. Our translators obviously knew what it meant—they translated it "go astray" in verse 23. They apparently chose "be ravished" to convey the play on words. This was a coordinated translation of several verses, using other passages so Bible readers would recognize two meanings of "ravished."

In Isaiah 13 and Zechariah 14, they used it to translate *shahgal*, and readers recognize by the context that "ravished" means the humbling of enslaved women after a military conquest. In Song of Solomon 4:9, they chose it to speak of the delights of marital love. And they used it here in Proverbs 5:19, where poetic Hebrew wording would bring both meanings to the mind of a Hebrew reader, to create a play on words in English to parallel the Hebrew.

When we get the full picture here, we see that Solomon is not instructing his son to enjoy pleasure for pleasure's sake. He tells him that by doing so, he binds himself to his wife. Solomon uses creative wording so that his son, when reflecting on it, will understand that he enjoys pleasure for a greater unity in a stronger marriage, and for protecting against temptation.

God does not want His people to forsake the pleasures of marital intimacy—He wants them to enjoy them. But He also wants us to understand that pleasure is not the goal, but (as we saw in Psalm 45), it is a means to an end.

Pleasure is strong, but it is to be our servant, not our master. When we use it for God's purposes, our delight in the pleasures He gives is God-honoring, joyous, and spiritually beneficial. When we pursue it for its own sake, whether in intimacy or in other aspects of our life, we make pleasure into a cruel and destructive master, destroying and perverting God's wonderful gifts in this life.

It is God's desire that through all the stages of marriage, with the ups and downs, epic lovers will always find joy, hope, and love in their relationship as they submit to the ongoing, infilling experience of the Spirit. The love expressed in epic lovers' relationship has the power to release rapturous expressions to make the journey reflect the image of God.

REVIEW QUESTIONS

1. Do you believe that true God-honoring pleasure protects couples against the temptations of counterfeit pleasures? Explain how.

2. What was it that the writer wanted to express, for which he chooses the Hebrew word *shahgah* for ravish?

3. What was Solomon's intention for sharing this verse with his son?

4. What is your understanding of the role of the wife from these words, "always with her love?"

5. How can this text preserve marital fidelity?

END NOTES

[1] Sheri Myers, *Chatting or Cheating: How to Detect Infidelity, Rebuild Love, and Affair-Proof Your Relationship* (Tarzana, CA: From the Heart Media, 2012).

[2] *Commentary on the Old Testament in Ten Volumes* by C.F. Keil and F. Delitzsch, *Volume VI: Proverbs, Ecclesiastes, Song of Solomon* by F. Delitzsch, translated from German by M.G. Easton (Grand Rapids: Eerdmans Publishing), Proverbs 5:18-20.

[3] The Bible: James Moffatt translates the last two lines: "…let her breasts give you rapture, and let her love ever ravish you." See "Putting Holy Fire in Your Marriage Stirring up Marital Passion." *http://www.net-burst.net/help/marriage.htm*.

The EPIC MARRIAGE

CONCLUSION

Epic marriage couples, seek to live their lives daily in ways to model and display the image/character of God in their relationships. The image/character of God is reflected through the demonstration of the fruit of love, which is expressed in five different ways. Epic couples view their marriage as a discipleship love lab, where every day their lives bear fruit of love as a testimony of the kingdom of God.

Adam, the first human being, was created possessing the fruit of love when the breath of God entered his body and he "became a living soul" (Genesis 2:7 KJV). From his loving body, God took a rib and created Eve, and then He placed them to live in the Garden of Eden. God blessed them and said, "… be fruitful" (Genesis 1:27). To be fruitful is a loaded statement!

There is much discussion in the theological schools of thought whether this text was a command God gave them or part of a blessing. We will leave the discussion to the theologians and other scholars, and we will interpret the text as written.

In the text, God instructed Adam and Eve to go "be fruitful." He simply instructed them to go practice, display, and develop the love that was deposited in them at their creation.

We believe that instruction was God's first and foremost intention for the first couple as well as all other married couples.

Many theologians and scholars would suggest that the text was an instruction to them to be fruitful by having children. This interpretation would surely go against the natural law of fruit bearing. First, before any fruit-bearing tree can reproduce itself, it must first bear fruit. Second, to have good quality fruit for reproduction, the fruit-bearing tree needs to go through a five-stage process: (1) the chilling hours, (2) pollination, (3) direct sunlight, (4) adequate water, and (5) fertilization. Like love, all five steps are required to produce whole, healthy, and sweet fruit. The seeds that experience the five stages are now ready to be planted to bring forth other fruit-bearing trees.

Just before we end this section, let us look a little further at the Hebrew word, "*parah*," phonetic spelling: (paw-raw'), which means "to bear fruit, or be fruitful." The message is clear: God said, "bear [grow] fruit [love] and then multiply" [bear children]. He did not say, multiply and be fruitful. God was more interested in character: quality (fruit) development before quantity—number increase.

After epic couples say, "I do," they usually leave the ceremony and reception to go on their honeymoon to start practicing and living in a loving and fruit-bearing relationship.

We all got married with the intention of practicing love and growing in love. It is out of love that we choose to multiply. We were like Adam and Eve, we left our marriage ceremonies, empowered by the Spirit, and charged with love chemicals washing our brains to go and demonstrate the fruit of love.

At the creation of the human being, the Holy Spirit resided within Adam and Eve. They were Spirit-empowered lovers. They were instructed to be side-by-side partners, connecting love and to serve each other in and through love. While Adam and Eve lived in love without sin, they

Conclusion

enjoyed the paradise of Eden and the full benefits of a perfect marriage.

Sin marred and destroyed the loving relationship between Adam, Eve, and God. They lost the intimate indwelling presence and fellowship of the Holy Spirit. Hence, Christ, the second Adam, came to restore the indwelling presence, the partnership petition, and the pure love of God, which leads to compassionate service in our marriages.

In the life to come, when there is no sin, death, or Satan, there will be another perfect marriage—the marriage of the Lamb to the bride, the Church.

In that perfect union, the Spirit of God will rule, where there will be partnership rule and loving service for all eternity. Until then, the epic marriage will serve as a replica, a model of the original Edenic design, and a foretaste of the heavenly marriage.

As marriage and family specialists, we are so thankful for the rich resources available to churches, couples, and families to provide personal and corporate education, as well as therapy and counseling for marriage and family. Many of our resources, therapies, and counseling are helpful, but we want to remind epic married couples, the best marital help and guide is allowing or submitting to the Spirit of God to lead. The key to living a victorious and successful epic marriage is submitting our lives afresh to Him every day. As we do that, we spend time engaging the Word of God and praying together, then He releases whatever is needed to be the lover we need to be.

The EPIC MARRIAGE

The Spirit-Empowered Life

ANSWER SHEET

CHAPTER 1

EPIC LOVERS' MARRIAGE
REVIEW QUESTIONS/ANSWERS

1. What are the characteristics of an "epic married couple"?
   (1) **Demonstrate humble hearts governed by love.**
   (2) **Execute deeds to exemplify and glorify God.**
   (3) **Personify godly standards that are esteemed by the Word of God, empowered by the Spirit of God, and revered by the Spirit-filled community of faith.**

2. What is the main message of Ephesians 5:18 given to married couples?
   That Christian couples need to allow their relationship to be filled and governed by the Spirit of God, instead of the good spirit of this world that overtakes and replaces the Spirit of God and can lead couples in the wrong lifestyles.

3. List the EPIC acrostic.
   E – Empowerment Encourager
   P – Prayer Partner
   I – Intimate Investor
   C – Compassionate Caregiver

4. According to a data report about divorce, what are two preventers of divorce?
   (1) **Premarital Counseling**
   (2) **Prayer**

5. Showing unconditional love requires a willingness to invest four things. They are:
   (1) **Time**
   (2) **Money**
   (3) **Energy**
   (4) **Patience**

CHAPTER 2

EPIC MARRIAGE FOUNDATION
REVIEW QUESTIONS/ANSWERS

1. List three blessings that should be ascertained before the consummation of an epic marriage.
   a. **God's blessing.**
   b. **The blessings of the church leaders and community of faith.**
   c. **The blessings and support of parents, family, and friends.**

2. In what ways do couples build their marital relationships on shifting ground?
   a. **They bring wounded self-images.**
   b. **Psychological and emotional scars.**

Answer Sheet

    c. Trauma and a faulty understanding of love and genuine commitment dynamics.

3. Why is faith in the God of the Bible so foundational to a strong and epic marriage?

4. Fill in the blank and explain the statement. Marriage is not simply an **event** but a **process.**

5. List the three elements of a Spirit-filled, marital foundation, and discuss why a person needs to master them prior to entering marriage?
    a. **Love for God.**
    b. **Love of self.**
    c. **Love for others.**

6. List and discuss the four kinds of marriages.
    a. **The Perfect Marriage**
    b. **The False Marriage**
    c. **The Fairytale Marriage**
    d. **The Real Marriage**

7. In real marriages, couples commit themselves to:
    a. **Show *respect* to each other.**
    b. **Be *empathetic* to each other.**
    c. ***Adapt* to their growth.**
    d. **Fully commit to grow in *love*.**

CHAPTER 3

**A LOVE PROMISE WORTH KEEPING!
REVIEW QUESTIONS/ANSWERS**

1. Scott Stanley, relationship expert, describes commitment as "a dedicated choice to give up other

competing choices." Explain! **It is commitment that keeps the relationship together, whether you feel like staying in the marriage or not.**

2. Is it true that commitment is something an individual has complete control over and can decide how it will be put into action? Explain! ***My Life or My Wife*, is an excellent example of how commitment in marriage is put into action on a daily basis.**

3. Fill in the blank. Commitment is "the part of the relationship that provides, **(safety and security)**, so couples can express their **(thoughts, feelings and desires openly).**

4. Fill in the blanks. Commitment acts like the **glue** that forges a bond between the couple to support them to navigate their way through the **rough patches.**

5. How did commitment make a difference in Dr. McQuilkin's story? **Commitment gave Dr. McQuilkin strength to endure life's difficulty during his wife's sickness and death.**

CHAPTER 4

COMMUNICATING IN LOVE
REVIEW QUESTIONS/ANSWERS

1. Fill in the blank. Effective communication understands the words, **(emotions, body language, and the tone)** behind the information that is being transferred.

Answer Sheet

2. Is it true that effective communication can facilitate therapeutic healing and renewal for couples? Please explain! **By following the tips of effectively listening, it will minimize and maximize couples' stress.**

3. What are the effects of talking or interrupting a speaker in the communication process? **It shows disrespect to the speaker and it can lead to misunderstanding of what is being communicated.**

4. According to Mace, what happens at the "experimental action stage"? ***Information is shared, Knowledge is gained, Insight is received. It leads to action and influences behavior change.***

5. Should a listener consider what is "said and felt" when replying to a speaker? Explain your answer. **Yes, because they are part and parcel of the communication process.**

CHAPTER 5

DIAMOND LOVE: CREATIVE USE OF CONFLICT REVIEW QUESTIONS/ANSWERS

1. What is the root cause of conflict? **It is differences.**

2. What is conflict? **It is a disagreement *heated-up*.**

3. How does conflict help an epic lover? **It increases personal growth, enhances communication between the couple, and builds the character of God in couples' lives.**

The EPIC MARRIAGE

4. What are a few things that cause an iceberg conflict? **Unresolved issues from the past, hidden expectations, self-perceptions, and self-esteem can cause conflict.**

5. What role does emotional awareness play in conflict management? **It helps to manage all one's feelings appropriately.**

CHAPTER 6

JOYFUL OR HAPPY LOVERS
REVIEW QUESTIONS/ANSWERS

1. Explain the difference between happiness and joy. **Happiness is based on circumstances, and joy is a fruit of the Spirit, a state of mind, and an orientation of the heart that is released by God.**

2. How is joy received? **It is a gift of the Spirit.**

3. How does an epic lover maintain joy in the marriage? **They know they have the indwelling Spirit with them. They trust in the Word of God and are committed to enjoying the ride by keeping their joy alive as they trust and rely upon Jesus Christ.**

4. What are two roadblocks of joy? **Negatively biased and conditioned**

5. Fill in the blank. Happiness is determined by (**circumstances**) and joy is (**a state of mind**).

Answer Sheet

CHAPTER 7

THE FEARLESS LOVER: (MACHO SEXUAL FULFILLMENT) REVIEW QUESTIONS/ANSWERS

1. What is ED? **A sexual dysfunction.**

2. Is ED a dysfunction of only older men? **No**

3. What can men do to control ED? **They can commit to changing their lifestyle by losing excess weight, increasing physical activity, eating healthier, getting adequate sleep, rest, and exercise. Also, they can seek professional help to design lifestyle changes and provide a system to monitor their changes.**

4. What are the effects of ED when it goes untreated? **It leads to impotence.**

5. What is the ABC Solomonic Love and Sex Model? **It is appreciation, benevolence, and consummation**

Chapter 8

THE DELICATE LOVER: (Designed to Be ... a Godly and Sensuous Woman) REVIEW QUESTIONS/ANSWERS

1. How did Webster's dictionary define *sensuous*? **"Pertaining to the senses; appealing to the senses, alive to the pleasure to be received through the senses."**

2. What are the three main reasons given for women's lack of or low sexual desires? **They are: (1) a feeling of unattractiveness, (2) lack of excitement, and (3) low overall satisfaction in life.**

3. Discuss the importance of estrogen and dopamine in relationship to a woman's sex drive? **Dopamine is a neurotransmitter that fuels sexual desire to rise in response to anticipation and excitement. Estrogen, on the other hand, provides an essential role in the growth and development of female secondary sexual characteristics.**

4. What can women learn from the Shulamite to improve their marriage? **She was receptive, courageous and uninhibited, candid and real, and communicative and sensuous.**

5. Discuss how important body image is to women's sexuality? **A poor body image does not just inhibit sexual desires in women—but it can hijack the view of their entire sexuality.**

CHAPTER 9

RAVISHING LOVERS
REVIEW QUESTIONS/ANSWERS

1. Do you believe that true God-honoring pleasure protects couples against the temptations of counterfeit pleasures? Explain how. **Pleasure is strong, but it is to be our servant, not our master. When we use it for God's purposes, our delight in the pleasures He gives is God-honoring, joyous, and spiritually beneficial. When we pursue it**

for its own sake, whether in intimacy or in other aspects of our lives, we make pleasure into a cruel and destructive master, destroying and perverting God's wonderful gifts in this life.

2. What was it that the writer wanted to express, for which he chooses the Hebrew word *shahgah* for ravish? **It appears that the use of *shah-gah*, so close to *shah-gal*, in a passage using very direct language to describe physical intimacy in marriage; it is intentional. This is poetic language with unusual wording to give one meaning while also bringing another word to mind—a pun, a play on words. The point of poetic or picturesque wording is to cause a reader to reflect, and in this case, the author wants his readers to reflect on both meanings. Solomon used *shahgah* in a way never used elsewhere, to bring *shahgal* to the mind of a Hebrew reader and thus convey these God-ordained purposes for pleasure in marital intimacy.**

    Solomon uses creative wording so that his son, when reflecting on it, will understand that he enjoys pleasure for a greater unity in a stronger marriage, and for protecting against temptation.

3. What was Solomon's intention for sharing this verse with his son? **Pleasure is strong, but it is to be our servant, not our master. When we use it for God's purposes, our delight in the pleasures He gives is God-honoring, joyous, and spiritually beneficial. When we pursue it for its own sake,**

whether in intimacy or in other aspects of our lives, we make pleasure into a cruel and destructive master, destroying and perverting God's wonderful gifts in this life.

4. What is your understanding of the role of the wife from these words, "always with her love?" **Wives are to make themselves available to their husband's love.**

5. How can this text preserve marital fidelity? **The text will preserve marital fidelity when both husbands and wives give of themselves totally to each other as unto the Lord.**